Armour, Weapons, *and* Warfare

A Scriptural Look at the Spiritual Instruments of Survival

Robert E. Daley

The Larry Czerwonka Company
Hilo, Hawai

First Edition

Published by: The Larry Czerwonka Company
Printed in the United States of America

ISBN: 0615773281
ISBN-13: 978-0615773285

Contents

Books by Robert E. Daley

From Everlasting To Everlasting

Raptures and Ressurections

Short Tales

So . . . What Happens to the Package?

Surviving Destruction as a Human Being

The New Testament - Pauline Revelation

The New Testament - Pauline Revelation Companion

The Gospel of John

What Color Are You?

What Makes a Christian Flaky?

What Really Happened to Judas Iscariot?

Who YOU Are In Christ . . . RIGHT NOW!

The Enhancement Series

#1 Book of Ecclesiastes

#2 Book of Daniel

#3 Book of Romans

#4 Book of Galatians

#5 Book of Hebrews

The Deeper Things of God Series

#1 The Personage of God

#2 The Personage of Man

#3 The Personage of Christ

Introduction

This book is a result of eight months of Bible study. It is designed to show the believer that he/she is more than a conqueror with the aid of the Holy Spirit.

Too many Christians live a defeated life because they do not know the Weapons of Heaven available to them as a result of their choice to become a New Creation. They do not know the parts of the Armour of God available to them for their protection and how to use them.

They are also not aware of the Weapons of Hell. If we can recognize when the enemy comes to 'steal, kill and destroy' us, we will be able to defeat him.

It is our prayer that when you finish reading this book you will read it again and rise up **loving** as a child of the living God and defeat the enemy when he comes to "blow your house down."

---

* all Bible quotes are from the King James Version

The Armour of God

"(For the weapons of our warfare are not carnal, but mighty through God to the pulling down of strong holds:)"
(II Corinthians 10:4)

As children of the Most High God, we find ourselves in a war. *(We most probably did not anticipate being drafted into a war when we made a decision to accept Jesus Christ of Nazareth as our personal Savior.)* Nevertheless, we now find ourselves as combatants in a real spiritual war.

"Ye are all the children of light, and the children of the day: we are not of the night, nor of darkness,

Therefore let us not sleep, as do others; but let us watch and be sober." (I Thessalonians 5:5-6)

Because the spiritual war that we are in is indeed a real war, we need to be sober-minded and not approach spiritual issues frivolously.

The enemy knows what he is doing, and he has had literally billions of people to practice on over the centuries. Since the enemy's only goal is to steal, and to kill, and to destroy, it is truly a life-and-death struggle. We must become pro-active in the position that we are to take and in any dealings that we might have with him.

God has provided us with good defense protection so that the enemy cannot prevail **if** we utilize that provided protection, and additionally, effectively operate our offensive weaponry. And in doing so, that we may move forward, gain ground, and take back what the enemy may have thus far successfully stolen.

Shall we then take the opportunity to examine the Armour of God that has been given unto us for our defense?

"Wherefore take unto you the whole armour of God, that ye may be able to withstand in the evil day, and having done all, to stand.

Stand therefore, having your loins girt about with truth, and having on the breastplate of righteousness;

And your feet shod with the preparation of the gospel of peace;

Above all, taking the shield of faith, wherewith ye shall be able to quench all the fiery darts of the wicked.

And take the helmet of salvation, and the sword of the Spirit, which is the word of God:" *(Ephesians 6:13-17)*

We shall begin our study with Scriptural clarity: ALL FIVE PIECES OF THE ARMOUR OF GOD ARE **METAPHORIC**. That is correct.

You cannot literally strap on the *belt of truth* around you as you might strap on a sash or a cummerbund.

You cannot slip on the *breastplate of righteousness* over your head as you would a blouse or a T-shirt, and then adjust the straps.

You cannot ease your feet into the *preparation of the gospel of peace* as you would normally step into a pair of house slippers or boots.

You cannot simply lift up the defensive *shield of faith* in front of you as if it were a forged piece of metal.

And, you cannot place the *helmet of salvation* upon your head as you would don a fedora or a bonnet and secure the chin-strap.

The Apostle Paul is speaking in a metaphoric manner. Giving for an illustration of solid spiritual reality, tangible physical articles so that the people of those days would be able to relate the very real spiritual instruments to articles that would be commonplace and well known.

May we examine each article and understand how we might clothe ourselves with the genuine protection provided by God.

(1) LOINS GIRT ABOUT WITH TRUTH

"Sanctify them through thy truth: thy word is truth." *(John 17:17)*

This declaration is a portion of a discourse of prayer that Jesus of Nazareth spoke as he was with his disciples and ministering to them at the Last Supper. It is indeed a declarative statement of accuracy.

The word of God is the absolute truth concerning all things, and anything that is presented out-of-line with what the word of God reveals and declares, is a lie. There can be, and is, only one truth.

We utilize this piece of armour, and *put it on* by learning what the actual truth is, in any given area, and then speaking forth the truth at every opportunity.

The protection that this piece of armour affords is the direct covering of the Holy Spirit of Truth Himself.

"Then said Jesus to those Jews which believed on him, If ye continue in my word, then are ye my disciples indeed;

And ye shall know the truth, and the truth shall make you free." *(John 8:31-32)*

Truth is not subject to any personal perceptions or individual points of view. Truth is not subject to what may be thought of by many as good intentions. Truth is not variable nor is it based upon what *I believe* . . . Truth is truth.

"I have not written unto you because ye know not the truth, but because ye know it, and that no lie is of the truth." *(I John 2:21)*

What does the Word of God have to say on any given subject?

What does the Word say about Mankind?
What does the Word say about Sin?

What does the Word say about Salvation?
What does the Word say about Marriage?
What does the Word say about Sex?
What does the Word say about the Origin of this planet?
What does the Word say about Food?
What does the Word say about God Himself?
What does the Word say about Behavior?
What does the Word say about Jesus?
What does the Word say about the Environment?
What does the Word say about Hell?
What does the Word say about Money?
What does the Word say about Business?
What does the Word say about Relationships?
What does the Word say about Creativity?

What does the Word of God have to say concerning any and all of these things?

The renewing of our mind involves the process of un-learning what the *experts* of the world that we live in have to say about the above mentioned subjects, and the re-learning of what the Word of God has to say about these very same subjects.

When that begins to occur, we will then be in the active process of renewing our mind, and the truth will prevail and protect us from projected lies and falsehood.

(2) BREASTPLATE OF RIGHTEOUSNESS

"By the word of truth, by the power of God, by the armour of righteousness on the right hand and on the left." (II Corinthians 6:7)

This second piece of armour is spoken of by the Apostle Paul to the Corinthian church, as well as to the believers in the city of Ephesus.

We utilize this piece of armour and <u>put it on</u> by actively walking in the light of God's written Word, and by choosing to obey His instructions in all things.

"But if we walk in the light, as he is in the light, we have fellowship one with another, and the blood of Jesus Christ his Son cleanseth us from all sin." (I John 1:7)

"Little children, let no man deceive you: he that doeth righteousness is righteous, even as he is righteous." (I John 3:7)

Righteousness has a power, or a ***force*** to it. There are two realities of righteousness, similar to there being two sharp edges on any specifically designed sword. The first sharp-edge is a position of legal righteousness.

Jesus of Nazareth was made to be sin that we might be made the righteousness of God in him. *(II Corinthians 5:21)* Today, if I am *in Christ* then I am legally righteous. It is not something that I have accomplished by myself . . . it is part of the exchange program of God that has been established through the finished work of Christ Jesus on the cross of Calvary.

However, the second sharp-edge reality of righteousness is on the practical side. This righteousness does concern my personal behavior.

I can be legally righteous by being *in Christ*, and yet be unrighteous in a practical manner because of my bad behavior. And that bad behavior cannot simply be ignored or undealt with. My behavior does matter. My unrighteous actions can nullify my *breastplate of righteousness* protection. If I do not purpose to walk righteously while I am on this Earth, there will be no practical cloak of righteousness to protect me.

"And if the righteous scarcely be saved, where shall the ungodly and the sinner appear?" (I Peter 4:18)

The **_righteous_** are individuals who have passed from spiritual death unto spiritual life. They are Born-Again. And as such are **legally** righteous because they are *in Christ*.

The **_sinner_** is an individual who remains spiritually dead. They are people who have never surrendered to becoming Born-Again within their spirit. They have no legal standing at all before a righteous God.

The **_ungodly_** are individuals who demonstrate unrighteous behavior consistent with this world's behavior . . . whether they are Born-Again Christians or not. They think like the world thinks, and they talk like the world talks, and they act like the world acts. This world is obviously ungodly, and they are also harmoniously ungodly in their behavior. For those who are begotten from above, their legal condition is not what is in question, but their practical behavior is. And an unrighteous, unsaved soul, can drag a legally saved spirit down into the bowels of Hell. The doctrine of **_Eternal Security_** cannot be Scripturally substantiated.

The assaults from wickedness within this world are very real. My actions must be just as real. This world is currently a whirlpool of sin and wickedness, and we are sadly caught in it and are swirling around, headed in a downward spiral.

God has thrown us a life-preserver with a rope attached to it from heaven in the person of Christ Jesus, to rescue us. And that life-preserver is available for whosoever will grab hold of it. That life-preserver is the only possibility that I have for rescue. However, my free-will choices dictate that I have a part to play.

"Whereby are given unto us exceeding great and precious promises: that by these ye MIGHT be partakers of the divine nature, having escaped the corruption that is in the world through lust." (II Peter 1:4)

". . . they themselves are the servants of corruption: for whom a man is overcome, of the same is he brought in bondage." (II Peter 2:19)

"Know ye not, that to whom ye yield yourselves servants to obey, his servants ye are to whom ye obey; whether of sin unto death, or of obedience unto righteousness?" *(Romans 6:16)*

In addition to my being *in Christ*, it boils down to my behavioral choices as well. If I behave righteously, then I am righteous in a practical manner; if I do not behave righteously, then I am not righteous in practical manner. And the question becomes dangerously clear . . . where shall I appear? *(I Peter 4:18)* It is that simple.

(3) PREPARATION OF THE GOSPEL OF PEACE

The third piece of armour that is mentioned is the feet shod with the *preparation of the gospel of peace*. According to the Apostle Paul *(Romans 1:16)* the gospel . . . or *good new'* . . . is the power of God unto salvation to everyone that believeth. The key to this piece of armour is the *preparation*.

We utilize this piece of armour, and <u>put it on</u> by learning who we are in Christ, and then being always ready to give an answer to every man that asks us the reason for the hope that they see in us. *(I Peter 3:15)*

Even within the Old Testament we see the Lord speaking through Isaiah the prophet, hundreds of years before the reality of the gospel ever came forth.

"How beautiful upon the mountain are the feet of him that bringeth good tidings, that publisheth peace; that bringeth good tidings of good, that publisheth salvation; that saith unto Zion, Thy God reigneth!" *(Isaiah 52:7)*

This entire world is in desperate need of rescue as we have just seen. While we hold fast to the life-preserver of salvation *in Christ*, we stretch forth our hands of ministration in a willingness to take the *good news* of the freely available life-preserver to others.

They in turn see the change that our life reflects, both legally and practically through our righteous behavior. And since the Word of God reveals to us that there is no peace to the wicked *(Isaiah 48:22)* we extend an arm of hope for them to respond to. However, we must remember that it works in conjunction with prayer. Without *effective* targeted prayer, our efforts will be futile.

"No man can come to me, except the Father which hath sent me draw him: and I will raise him up at the last day." *(John 6:44)*

* Please note that all of the pieces of armour that we are observing, find their foundation within the declared, written, Word of God. The second epistle of Peter reveals,

"According as his divine power hath given unto us all things that pertain unto life and godliness, through the knowledge of him that hath called us to glory and virtue." *(II Peter 1:3)*

(4) SHIELD OF FAITH

The fourth piece of spiritual protection is the *shield of faith*. This is not an article of clothing that we put on, but rather an instrument that we handle. We use this shield to block assaults that are launched at us by the enemy.

"Behold, his soul which is lifted up is not upright in him: but the just shall live by his faith." *(Habakkuk 2:4)*

"So then faith cometh *by hearing, and hearing by the word of* **God."** *(Romans 10:17)*

"For I say, through the grace given unto me, to every man that is among you, not to think of himself *more highly than he ought to think; but to think soberly, according as God hath dealt to every man the measure of faith." (Romans 12:3)*

"Fight the good fight of faith, lay hold on eternal life, whereunto thou art also called, and hast professed a good profession before many witnesses." (I Timothy 6:12)

"Now faith is the substance of things hoped for, the evidence of things not seen." (Hebrews 11:1)

"But without faith it is impossible to please him*: for he that cometh to God must believe that he is, and that he is a rewarder of them that diligently seek him." (Hebrews 11:6)*

Faith itself is a creative element. And because it has real substance to it God has molded it into a force field for our benefit.

We utilize this protective shield by choosing to place our trust in, and believe, what God has stated is so . . . in spite of what other evidence may present itself.

"For ever, O Lord, thy word is settled in heaven." (Psalm 119:89)

God has said it, and that settles it. The root of faith is the Word of God. And because the Word of God is a living substance, the faith that comes from it is alive as well.

Being free-will creatures we choose to place our confidence in what our God, who cannot lie, has whispered into our ear and borne witness to within our heart. His report is the report that we will choose to receive. A confidence develops that takes precedence over circum-stances. The report of the eye or the ear does not override the quiet confidence of *knowing* what truth has declared.

A natural man can have a *sense-knowledge faith,* and it is a real kind of faith. He can examine the evidence presented by his five physical senses and determine that the chair will hold his weight, before he attempts to sit down upon it. Over a period of time, he can even reach the point where he no longer feels the need to examine each and every chair that he considers sitting upon because he chooses to put a trust in the chair manufacturer, **believing** that the manufacturer knows what he is doing . . . so he just sits down. He reaches a place where he becomes virtually unconscious concerning the releasing of his *sense-knowledge faith* in the chair.

The Born-Again spiritual man needs to develop a *revelation* or *Bible faith.* God has designed that this is the kind of faith which resides within His **"quick and powerful and sharper than any two-edged sword"** word. *(Hebrews 4:12)* God will start a man off by giving him **the** measure of this kind of faith at his new birth, *(Romans 12:3)* but the man must increase his own amount of this faith by his own efforts. He does this by disciplining himself to read and meditate on, and study the Word of God regularly. (This is also known as the renewing of the mind.) *(Romans 12:2)*

Over a period of time, the man begins to cultivate a real trust in the manufacturer of life Himself, **believing** that the manufacturer of life knows what He is doing . . . so he simply acts on what the word of God says. He reaches a place where he becomes almost unconscious concerning the releasing of his faith in the dealing with all of the issues of life.

When we know the report of the Lord on any given issue, we then take the powerful Word of God and mix it together with the trust that we have cultivated in our God. We purpose to take our stand and speak forth and declare the Lord's report on any given issue, right in the face of whatsoever circumstances may be screaming at our eyes and ears at the time.

As the faith-filled utterance is emitted, an invisible force-field of confidence emerges with protective coverage.

(5) THE HELMET OF SALVATION

"But let us, who are of the day, be sober, putting on the breastplate of faith and love; and for an helmet, the hope of salvation." *(I Thessalonians 5:8)*

To the Thessalonians, the Apostle Paul reveals that our *breastplate* piece of armour also has the influence of faith and love. And he mentions that there is also hope connected to our *helmet of salvation.*

A helmet is used to protect the head, which is a vital part of our body. Our head is where our thinking processes take place. What is in our head is the operationally-key portion of our soul. *(Change what a man thinks and you will change what the man truly believes . . . Change what the man believes, and you will change what actually comes out of his mouth . . . Change what comes out of his mouth, and you will change what the man actually receives into his hands.)* Therefore, our head holds a position of importance and must be protected, particularly against falsehood and the traditions of men. We are New Testament New Creations, and it is imperative that we learn who we are *in Christ.* It is not optional if survival and victory are our goals.

We utilize this piece of the armour by becoming knowledgeable of, and fully persuaded concerning our position *in Christ*, and by learning fully who we now are in him.

"I am crucified with Christ: nevertheless I live; yet not I, but Christ liveth in me: and the life which I now live in the flesh I live by the faith of the Son of God, who loved me, and gave himself for me." *(Galatians 2:20)*

If not **the** biggest, then one of the biggest difficulties that modern Christianity suffers from is a lack of understanding and acceptance of this spiritual truth. And because this truth is not a reality within so many believers, they are swayed from day to day, and from situation to situation, as to what the outcome will be.

In Christ, we are more than conquerors. *In Christ*, all things are mine. *In Christ* nothing shall be impossible. *In Christ*, all principalities and powers are subject to me. *In Christ*, I am seated with authority in heavenly places. *In Christ*, I have been physically healed by the stripes that Jesus bore for me. *In Christ*, all of my needs shall be met, and God will grant unto me the desires of my heart. *In Christ*, I can do all things because he strengthens me. . . . and on and on and on.

"My people are destroyed for lack of knowledge: because thou hast rejected knowledge, I will also reject thee, that thou shalt be no priest to me: seeing thou hast forgotten the law of thy God, I will also forget thy children." (Hosea 4:6)

A lack of a genuine knowledge of who we are *in Christ* is prevalent within Christianity today. And God has told us clearly that destruction can lie directly ahead of us if we persist in our spiritual ignorance. And it is not God who will destroy us. The wicked one is the one who comes for no other reason but to steal and to kill and to destroy. He is the one who will destroy us because of our ignorance of the finished work of what God has done for us *in Christ*.

As a Born-Again Christian, we should not remain in a defensive attitude and position. We now have the advantage. Because of Christ Jesus we should be moving over to the offensive side of the team and taking back what the devil has stolen, both from our family and loved ones and even more so, that which is needed within our own lives.

Concerning that of which we have shared thus far, this is the sum:

1. We are to renew our minds so that we know what the truth is on any given subject. (i.e. the difference between that which is correct and that which is incorrect).

Belt of Truth.

2. We are to recognize that we are legally the righteousness of God *in Christ*, and with the help of the Holy Spirit we will be able to change our behavior.

Breastplate of Righteousness.

3. Genuinely now knowing who we are *in Christ*, we need to be ready to share that reality with every man who asks the reason for the hope that is within us.

Shoes of the Preparation of the Gospel of Peace.

4. Deciding to place our trust in God . . . who's report will we believe? Free-will choice is definitely involved and very important.

Shield of Faith.

5. We are to be fully knowledgeable and persuaded concerning our new legal position in Christ.

Helmet of Salvation.

These pieces of *Armour* are designed by God to be donned by every believer, and are never to be removed. They act as a continual protection against the assaults that the kingdom of darkness would launch.

We need to choose to take unto us ***"the whole armour of God"*** *(Ephesians 6:11)* that we may be able to withstand the attacks of Satan in the evil day, and having done all that we are capable of doing, to stand.

Every single believer is able to do this. But we must be pro-active. The protection of the armour does not just happen because we can quote the Scriptures.

The "Tools" of Christianity

"(For the weapons of our warfare are not carnal, but mighty through God to the pulling down of strongholds;)" (II Corinthians 10:4)

(1) THE WORD OF GOD

If we remain mindful of our original armour Scripture notation from the Apostle Paul's letter to the Ephesians, we find the *sword of the Spirit* is the last mentioned instrument. And it is clearly brought out that the *sword of the Spirit* is, in fact, the Word of God.

There is a dual application to that sword, that is many times missed by some. The **S** on the word spirit is capitalized which normally indicates to the reader that the Holy Spirit of God is the one who is being referenced. And indeed the Holy Spirit is the power that is wielded with the use of that sword.

However, a small **s** is what should be used because it is, in reality, the effective operating weapon that an individual's Born-Again, Human spirit has been given to obtain the desired victory.

All of the other pieces of armour have to do with a Human Being. When we get to the one offensive weapon that is being mentioned within the same set of Scriptures, and that is being given to men, we should not automatically shift over to the Personage of God. It is something that is also still of the Human Being.

". . . for thou hast magnified thy word above all thy name." (Psalm 138:2b)

At the time that the psalmist declared this truth the name of Jesus had not yet been given nor exalted. Nevertheless, at that time and even until now the word of God is still magnified above *"all thy name."*(Psalms 138:2b)

All that currently exists finds its foundation in the Word of God. The written word is the tangible substance that has been given unto us to utilize as an instrument, and it incorporates within it the spoken word.

"All things were made by him; and without him was not any thing made that was made." *(John 1:3)*

That, which has been creatively spoken, has emanated forth from that which is Living. When the written is received and infused by the Living abiding within, then that which is spoken will produce. And only Man has been privileged to house the Living within.

"For the word of God is quick, and powerful, and sharper than any two-edged sword, piercing even to the dividing asunder of soul and spirit, and of the joints and marrow, and is a discerner of the thoughts and intents of the heart." *(Hebrews 4:12)*

Nothing overrides the Word of God. Nothing is more powerful than the Word of God. Nothing is able to defeat the Word of God. Nothing is able to prevail against the Word of God. God has recorded His declarations, and that is that.

Should we choose to become people of the Word of God, we shall become the most formidable power on earth.

*   *   *

Illustrative wise, the Word of God is likened unto a Band-Aid. That Band-Aid has two adhesive strips on either side of the gauze pad. These two adhesive strips hold the Band-Aid in place until the necessary healing is able to manifest.

The two spiritual adhesive strips that God has attached to His word, so that it will work properly all the time, are *faith* and *patience*. We take the Word of God, which we choose to believe in our heart, and we apply it to any given situation . . . or to a person . . . or to an occurrence . . . or to a desire that we may have . . . or to our bodies . . . or to any other viable subject. Utilizing the words that we are privileged to speak, **we apply** the spiritual Band-Aid to the subject in question with the declared end-result declaration of the Word of God **with faith**. And then we exercise thankfulness, and **with *patience* we wait** for the manifestation.

We accompany the process with frequent spoken affirmations of the declared end-result declaration, in order to keep our mind, emotions, and free-will in line with truth. Expectation is the spiritual nectar of miracles, and so we cultivate it continually. The word prevails.

The Logos will become the Rhema . . . with time. We are the determining factor because God does not change, now or ever. The Logos begins within the mind. It is processed into the mind through reading. With continual rehearsal, a supernatural process will then occur which will cause the Logos to drop from the mind into the heart. Once in the heart, the *knower* picks it up to feed on. Life begets life, and at just the right time the Logos becomes Rhema and comes out of the mouth to accomplish the chosen desire.

The new Born-Again Human spirit is the repository where this transition takes place. The unchanging Word of God is what goes in. The unchanging Word of God is what comes out. The unchanging Word of God is what accomplishes the desire. The changeable determining factor in the process is the Born-Again Human spirit.

"For whom he did foreknow, he also did predestinate to be conformed to the image of his Son, that he might be the firstborn among many brethren." (Romans 8:29)

This conforming change is the work of the Holy Spirit of God now living within the Born-Again Human spirit. In the eons ahead we will think just like Jesus thinks . . . and talk just like Jesus talks . . . and act just like Jesus acts. And because of that, the Father in heaven can trust us to go anywhere within His created Universe and carry-out any given task assignment without flaw. *"Portable Jesus Units"* on assignment for our Father, to effect creative and maintenance changes, for the benefit of obedient moral creation.

(2) THE NAME OF JESUS

"Wherefore God also hath highly exalted him, and given him a name which is above every name:

That at the name of Jesus every knee should bow, of things in heaven, and things in earth, and things under the earth;

And that every tongue should confess that Jesus Christ is Lord, to the glory of God the Father." (Philippians 2:9-11)

The name of Jesus is the second most powerful weapon, or tool, that God has made available to us. Power finds its residence within a person. In the case of Jesus of Nazareth, when the unprecedented, spiritual, supernova explosion occurred within the bowels of this planet, that brought forth a New Creature into existence, the power that was needed to accomplish that event was encapsulated within the name of that New Creation that was risen from the dead.

The Logos name of Jesus will become the Rhema name of Jesus by the same process which applies to all of the Word of God. It must be gripped by the *knower* and become a reality.

The name of cancer is not higher than the name of Jesus. The name of leprosy is not higher, nor the name of emphysema, nor asthma, nor allergies, nor lupus, nor fibromyalgia, nor any other name. The name of Jesus is superior to them all, and various names representing rebellion as well as all other names that have been given, are to bow their knees to the command of Jesus.

"And these signs shall follow them that believe; In my name shall they cast out devils; they shall speak with new tongues;

They shall take up serpents; and if they drink any deadly thing, it shall not hurt them; they shall lay hands on the sick, and they shall recover." (Mark 16:17-18)

Supernova explosion power has now been handed over to those who are Born-Again and have become members of the household of God. New Creations *in Christ* are referred to as *believers* because we choose to believe. Every believer has been commissioned by Jesus to go forth into this world, take his power-filled name, and defeat the powers of darkness at every turn. We are to boldly use that name to deal with sickness and disease, demonic activity, and every discernable work of darkness.

Every prayer or petition presented to our Father in heaven receives audience when accompanied by that name. However, the name of Jesus can all too easily become little more than a postage stamp on a request or declaration if faith is not continually maintained in the reality of what has taken place. We must guard against that happening.

"And when Peter saw it, he answered unto the people, Ye men of Israel, why marvel ye at this? or why look ye so earnestly on us, as though by our own power or holiness we had made this man to walk?"

"And his name, through faith in his name, hath made this man strong, whom ye see and know: yea, the faith which is by him hath given him this perfect soundness in the presence of you all." (Acts 3:12, 16)

Here is a Biblical record of an early use of the name of Jesus. Please recognize that Peter knew that it was not because of them that this miracle occurred. And he knew that faith must accompany the use of Jesus' name. The name of Jesus is not designed to be something that is merely slapped on the end of a prayer to finish it up. Faith is necessary.

Today there is a large void of faith in operation. We are going through the motions, but we actually do not believe in what we are saying nor doing. Because if we honestly did believe in what we were saying and doing, we would not be continuing to ask again, and again, and again for the same thing. And we would not be acting in rote repetition over and over again concerning the things that we do.

The name of Jesus is beyond comparison, but it must be accompanied by faith, in order for it to work as God has designed it to work.

(3) THE BLOOD OF THE LAMB

"Much more then, being now justified by his blood, we shall be saved from wrath through him." (*Romans 5:9*)

"How much more shall the blood of Christ, who through the eternal Spirit offered himself without spot to God, purge your conscience from dead works to serve the living God."
(*Hebrews 9:14*)

The blood of the Lamb of God is the third of nine weapons or tools that our God has made available to us for survival and victory purposes.

The blood of Jesus is probably the most underrated and unused weapon that we have within our arsenal. The blood is usually talked about as something that came on the scene when it was needed, did the job that it was designed to do, and is now within the annals of the things of the past. Nothing could be further from the truth.

Within the Old Testament records, we find that a priesthood was required in order to have any dealings with the element of blood. Blood is incredibly important to God, and is the very vehicle that God has designed should carry the *force of life*. Animal blood is an undefiled blood that can be utilized, within the sanctioned priesthood of the Nation of Israel, to atone for and cover, sin and transgression for covenant individuals. Human blood is unfortunately defiled because of

Adam's sin and is unusable for anything. The blood of Jesus of Nazareth, because he was born of a virgin, without the aid of a Human father, is the only undefiled Human blood that was able to be used, by God, to destroy the power and the effects of sin.

Today, Peter reveals to us that we are **"a royal priesthood"**, *(1 Peter 2:9)* and as such we have a legal right to handle blood. Utilizing our own tongues as you would a paint brush, we are able to verbally apply the blood of Jesus to a particular person, or a situation, or an object for the purpose of protection. Christianity often declares "plead the blood" but usually how to do that is not clearly conveyed.

The blood of the Lamb of God is a very real and tangible substance and is a viable weapon made available for us to utilize. The applied blood of the risen New Creation Jesus will cause the powers of darkness to flee in terror. It is well known within the kingdom of darkness what the blood has soundly accomplished, and agents of that kingdom are terrified at the thought that the blood of the Lamb of God will be directed toward them.

It is well worth our time and effort to learn all that we can about this extremely powerful weapon.

(4) FAITH

"Now faith is the substance of things hoped for, the evidence of things not seen." *(Hebrews 11:1)*

Earlier within this study we looked at *the shield of faith (Ephesians 6:16)* as being part of the Armour of God that has been made available to us. And that shield is defensively viable and extremely powerful in its armour function and role.

However, faith is also a weapon, or more accurately a workable tool, within the toolbox of Christianity.

"But without faith it is impossible to please him: for he that cometh to God must believe that he is, and that he is a rewarder of them that diligently seek him." *(Hebrews 11:6)*

One of the things that we know for sure will please God is faith. We are admonished to *"walk by faith"* and not by sight, *(II Corinthians 5:7)* and even to *"live by faith"*. *(Romans 1:17, Galatians 3:11, Hebrews 10:38)*

One of the *adhesive strips* that accompanies the Band-Aid of the Word of God is faith. We must choose to put our trust in God, and what God declares, in any given situation, in spite of whatever else may be screaming at us, and contrary to the testimony of the word.

"So then faith cometh by hearing, and hearing by the word of God." *(Romans 10:17)*

Finally, there is only one way to increase *the measure* of faith that is given unto us *(Romans 12:3)* and that is by spending focused time in the Word of God. Faith will not increase by prayer, nor by singing and worship, nor by fasting, nor by anything other than spending focused time in the Word of God.

(5) THE BAPTISM OF THE HOLY SPIRIT

"But ye shall receive power, after that the Holy Ghost is come upon you: and ye shall be witnesses unto me both in Jerusalem, and in all Judea, and in Samaria, and unto the uttermost part of the earth." *(Acts 1:8)*

After the new birth takes place, every believer should want to be baptized with the Holy Spirit.

Because the Scriptures reveal unto us that the Holy Spirit of God came UPON Jesus at the time of his water baptism *(Luke 3:22)* and that Jesus himself said that the Holy Spirit would come UPON those that He would baptize, *(Acts 1:8)* we should cultivate a mental picture of the Holy Spirit coming upon us like a cloak. And that when that occurs we become enveloped and covered with dynamic power. We already have the Holy Spirit living on the inside of us because of the new birth, and

His promise to us is to never leave us nor forsake us. *(Hebrews 13:5)* However, it is the baptism, or the *cloaking* of the Holy Spirit that will make all the difference. That is where the power will come from that will accomplish the job. That is the power that will heal the sick. That is the power that will raise the dead. That is the power that will drive out demons. But, we are the ones on the inside of the cloak. We are the ones that carry the authority here on this earth. We are the ones who are to give the directives of what we would like to see happen. We are the ones in charge. We are the boss.

And we are not overriding God when we take up that kind of mindset and position of confidence. We are not arrogantly exalting ourselves above God. The Scriptures declare that, without God, we can do nothing. *(John 9:33 & 15:5)* We are the conduits through which God works here on this earth. We need to be willing to humble ourselves to God's instructions and God's plan and recognize that and put an end to projected false humility.

Jesus was cloaked with the Holy Spirit at the Jordan River, and he went about everywhere doing good by the power of God. Even he stated that it was the Father (by the power of the Holy Spirit . . . because He is the power portion of the Godhead) that doeth the works. *(John 14:10)*

So it will be with us as well. We need to boldly act upon what the Word of God instructs, and *trust* the power of the *cloak* to get the job done. Here are a few ways the Holy Spirit will help us:

a. Boldness —

"Now when they saw the boldness of Peter and John, and perceived that they were unlearned and ignorant men, they marvelled; and they took knowledge of them, that they had been with Jesus." *(Acts 4:13)*

Boldness comes with the Baptism of the Holy Spirit. Only a few short weeks before this event the disciples were hiding behind closed doors, afraid of being caught by those who hated Jesus. Now they are challenging those same powers that they had been hiding from. What made the difference? The cloaking power of the Holy Spirit.

We need that boldness in the day in which we live. These are the last days. The Scriptures reveal what kind of days these will be. If we are going to carry forth the gospel of the Lord Jesus so that none should perish, we are going to have to be bold. Bold in our thinking. Bold in our speaking. And, bold in our actions.

b. Power to be a witness —

"But ye shall receive power, after that the Holy Ghost is come upon you: and ye shall be witnesses unto me both in Jerusalem, and in all Judea, and in Samaria, and unto the uttermost part of the earth." *(Acts 1:8)*

There is a large difference between *witnessing* and *being a witness*. A person's life can be very questionable, and, in fact, one does not even need to be Born-Again in order to *witness* for the gospel. A person can pass out tracts, knock on doors, stand on street corners, or be involved in any number of activities that may be thought of as *witnessing*.

However, living correctly and walking in the light as he is in the light presents a powerful *witness* of the reality of a living God and a changed life. And when Jesus addressed his disciples on the Mount of Olives, just before his return to heaven, that is exactly what he was talking about. The Holy Spirit baptism gives us the power to live holy and to live right. Every believer should desire that.

c. Active working of the Spirit of Truth —

"Howbeit when he, the Spirit of truth, is come, he will guide you into all truth: for he shall not speak of himself; but whatsoever he shall hear, that shall he speak: and he will show you things to come." *(John 16:13)*

"We are of God: he that knoweth God heareth us; he that is not of God heareth not us. Hereby know we the spirit of truth, and the spirit of error." (I John 4:6)

The same author speaks to us about truth in two venues. We have a promise that the Holy Spirit will lead us into all truth. And we have the discernment to distinguish between truth and error. The same Holy Spirit does both.

This author is persuaded that the Baptism of the Holy Spirit is the door opener to the Gifts of the Holy Spirit that we see in I Corinthians Chapter 12.

It is manifest in the days in which we live, that the majority of individuals that claim identification with Christ are not baptized in the Holy Spirit . . . even though Jesus commanded that it should take place. Sadly, because of that, we miss out on many things that God has for us to be victorious and successful in while we are on this earth, and the world suffers for it as well.

d. Revelation insight —

"Howbeit when he, the Spirit of truth, is come, he will guide you into all truth: for he shall not speak of himself; but whatsoever he shall hear, **that** *shall he speak: and he will show you things to come."* (John 16:13)

The Holy Spirit will *guide* us into all truth. Because of the new birth, we are spoken of as being children of light in a world of darkness. We are in the process of *feeling* our way through this darkness, and are in need of the One who knows the way through this labyrinth unto the truth, to help us.

He will *impress* upon our consciousness an idea or a notion or an insight that goes contrary to the prevalent darkness. That is the process of taking our hand and leading us into the accuracy of the light, if we are willing to go.

In addition, He will *"show us things to come"*. He already knows about all of the tomorrows that are lined up at the front door. And we have His word that He will *reveal* things to come. Being a child of God puts us on the cutting edge and a step ahead of the remainder of the world, if we are able to learn how to tune in. The growth development of the fruit of our new Born-Again, recreated, Human spirit is that process of tuning in.

e. Memory —

"But the Comforter, which is the Holy Ghost, whom the Father will send in my name, he shall teach you all things, and bring all things to your remembrance, whatsoever I have said unto you." *(John 14:26)*

This is another Scripture verse that verifies the Trinity . . . Three Persons in One God. {the Holy Ghost, the Father, and my name (Jesus)}.

The Baptism of the Holy Spirit affords us the assurance of needed remembrance. It is believed by some that God has given unto Man the gift of a complete photographic memory capacity. The brain records all of the data input that comes into it from the five physical senses. Man's ability to draw from that complete record and download the data is affected by sin and the distractions of this world.

Upon the completion of the *conforming to his image* process, *(Romans 8:29)* we shall ultimately think just like Jesus thinks and have perfect recall. The Word of God will have washed all of the undesirable influence of this Probational Period into the annals of forgetfulness. The Word of God will be the very foundation of all of our thinking.

However, we do not have to wait until the sweet by-and-by arrives to enjoy this. We can depend upon the Holy Spirit, to bring to our attention, right here and right now, the Word of God, at every instance that it is needed.

f. Open the door to the Gifts of the Holy Spirit —

"Now there are diversities of gifts, but the same Spirit.
And there are differences of administrations, but the same
Lord.
And there are diversities of operations, but it is the same God
which worketh all in all." (I Corinthians 12:4-6)

The empowering Baptism of the Holy Spirit was not designed by God to be some sort of spiritual dessert that believers can choose to pass-up because they are full from their spiritual dinner and are watching their weight. It is an incredible granting, from heaven, to aid all believers in their spiritual responsibilities that each one of us have while they are here on this earth.

Every New Creation that qualifies for ruling and reigning with Christ, and is granted the responsibilities that go with that regency, shall be baptized with the Holy Spirit.

However, while we are still on this earth, and the probation continues, there is a job that still needs to be done and we do not have all the tools within ourselves to get that job done. So the Holy Spirit of God has gifts of wisdom, and knowledge, and super-natural faith and healings, and miracles, and prophetical declarations, and spiritual discernment, and various tongues, and interpretations to go with those tongues, in order to get that job done.

God's focus is on the people that are choosing to distance themselves from Him. His focus is not on the fine houses, nor slick cars, nor exciting television shows or movies, nor on the stock market, nor the price of gasoline, nor on the cost of living, nor on the weather, nor on politics, nor on anything else that is going to pass away within the not-to-distant future. His focus is on people. People have been designed to last forever, all of the other topics that are named above are not.

As believers, we are supposed to be becoming more and more tuned-in to spiritual things with each passing day. This author is persuaded that the Baptism of the Holy Spirit opens the door to the flowing of and operation of the gifts that the Holy Spirit desires to grant unto Mankind for the purpose of reconciliation of all men.

g. Rivers of Living Water —

"In the last day, that great day of the feast, Jesus stood and cried, saying, If any man thirst, let him come unto me, and drink.

He that believeth on me, as the Scripture hath said, out of his belly shall flow rivers of living water.

(But this spake he of the Spirit, which they that believe on him should receive: for the Holy Ghost was not yet given; because that Jesus was not yet glorified.)". *(John 7:37-39)*

The gospel of John was written decades after Jesus was risen from the dead and had ascended into heaven, thus the parenthesis. As long as Jesus was walking among men, he was their provider and their comforter. He was empowered and directed by the Holy Spirit in all that he did because he was without sin . . . but he was the only one.

He is referencing the manifestation of *"the promise of the Father"* that he had told the disciples about. *(Acts 1:4)*

The Baptism of the Holy Spirit became possible when men were brought to a sin-free condition, through the new birth, that the Holy Spirit Himself accomplished. And now He wants to empower and direct each believer into victory and success in every endeavor in life.

Flowing rivers of living water directly refers to an unending utterance potential that the Holy Spirit will cause to rise up from within the core of our newly recreated Human spirit.

(6) SPEAKING WITH OTHER TONGUES

"For he that speaketh in an unknown tongue speaketh not unto men, but unto God: for no man understandeth him; howbeit in the spirit he speaketh mysteries." *(I Corinthians 14:2)*

*"He that speaketh in an unknown tongue edifieth himself;
but he that prophesieth edifieth the church."* (I Corinthians 14:4)

Speaking in an unknown tongue is a tool or a weapon within its own right.

This Scripture reveals that speaking in an unknown tongue is speaking unto God Himself on a one-to-one basis. And at least one of the benefits is that the person who chooses to do this builds himself up spiritually, even though he may not know exactly how that happens.

The context of these verses puts us within a church setting. A gathering together of the local saints for a time of worship and edification. But the same truths will apply and operate on an *at home* or *on the job* setting as well.

The spirit of the New Creation man is now alive. The once severed communication umbilical has again been restored. God, the Holy Spirit, is now residing within the man's personage, via the finished adoptive work of the cross. God will once again begin to communicate to the man from within, speaking primarily in a still, small voice, and quoting His written word.

Without the baptism of the Holy Spirit, any Born-Again man is able to speak back unto God, but within the limited usage of his own spoken language, and to the depth of whatever his awareness of the details of the given situation may be. And let us not be naive, we are in a war; and you can be sure that the devil will have his communication

operators listening in on the conversation to find out what the man knows.

With the baptism of the Holy Spirit, and the God-given evidence of speaking in an unknown tongue, the man is able to speak back unto God in a *private conversation* that is not able to be tapped into by the minions of Hell. And, the Holy Spirit knows all of the details of the given situation and is able to intercede and present the petition unto God the Father with precise accuracy.

"For with stammering lips and another tongue will he speak to this people.

To whom he said, This is *the rest* wherewith *ye may cause the weary to rest; and this* is *the refreshing: yet they would not hear."* (Isaiah 28:11-12)

"In the law it is written, With men of *other tongues and other lips will I speak unto this people; and yet for all that will they not hear me, saith the Lord."* *(I Corinthians 14:21)*

God Himself announced the phenomenon of speaking with other tongues hundreds of years before it was manifest. And the Apostle Paul expounds upon what Isaiah had prophesied, and further states:

"Wherefore tongues are for a sign, not to them that believe, but to them that believe not:" *(I Corinthians 14:2)*

In addition to being extremely helpful in our own prayer life, and the strengthening of our faith, and our being able to communicate privately with God . . . tongues have been designed, by God, to be *a sign.*

In the days of Jesus, men were asking all the time *"show us a sign" "show us a sign".* *(Luke 11:29)* And now in our day we have been given something from God that God Himself says will be *a sign* to them that believe not, and many choose not to use it. May the God of all grace help us to see what we are doing.

Even so Lord Jesus, come quickly.

(7) PRAYER

"And in that day ye shall ask me nothing. Verily, verily, I say unto you, Whatsoever ye shall ask the Father in my name, he will give it *you."* *(John 16:23)*

"Therefore I say unto you, What things soever ye desire, when ye pray, believe that ye receive them, and ye shall have them.

And when ye stand praying, forgive, if ye have aught against any; that your Father also which is in heaven may forgive you your trespasses.

But if ye do not forgive, neither will your Father which is in heaven forgive your trespasses." (Mark 11:24-26)

Prayer is a privilege that God has afforded to Human Beings to be able to co-operate with Him in fulfilling His Divine Plan.

We desire something, or need to have something done, and we petition God through prayer to achieve that goal.

And, as the Scripture reveals, it is not something that is simply based upon what we may want or need. Forgiveness and Unforgiveness are powerful spiritual positions. Genuine forgiveness will open wide the doors of response and fulfillment. And just as powerfully, unforgiveness will stand as an iron wall, barrier, to thwart desire.

". . . The effectual fervent prayer of a righteous man availeth much.

Elijah was a man subject to like passions as we are, and he prayed earnestly that it might not rain: and it rained not on the earth by the space of three years and six months.

And he prayed again, and the heaven gave rain, and the earth brought forth her fruit." (James 5:16b-18)

Answer to prayer is not based upon numbers. It is not a matter of how many individuals one can gather together to collectively assail heaven. Prayer does not find its basis in democracy. "We all just voted yes Lord, so grant our request".

There is the validity of the law of agreement within the parameters of prayer. Jesus himself told us that it would only require the genuine agreement of two, but there must be true agreement and not just hope for that petition to be effective.

Elijah was a single individual, and yet his request was heard and granted. That is because Elijah was a man who knew his God. Elijah was a man who knew what his God could do. Elijah was a man who believed that his God heard him. And Elijah was a man who believed that his God would do whatever he asked him to do.

Prayer is, after all, a request from one who is unable, to One who certainly is able, to accomplish a specific task.

For prayer to be effective, it needs to be based upon the Word of God.

". . . yet ye have not, because ye ask not.

Ye ask, and receive not, because ye ask amiss, that ye may consume it upon your lusts." *(James 4:2b-3)*

What we ask God to do must be in line with what He has already declared. God has shared with us just what is so within this Universe. Sinful men have taken it upon themselves to develop their own perspectives and cultivate their own thoughts as to what is what and how things work, but that does not make it so. God is the designer and the manufacturer, and as such, He is the only One who truly knows how it all works.

We can learn the *"ways of God"* as Moses did. *(Psalms 103:7)* And we can learn how God thinks through a focused knowledge and understanding of His word. The word of God is the foundation for everything that takes place.

The answer that we desire from our God should be the focal point of our petition, not the problem. Too many times we elaborate to God what the problem is, when the truth is, He already knows what the problem is. We go on and on and on describing the details of the difficulty because that is where our focus is. We exercise and release more faith in the problem than we do in the solution. The problem becomes bigger within our mind than the God who can solve it.

We need to know what the solution is so that we may release our faith in line with what God has declared.

(8) HOLY ANGELS

"Are they not all ministering spirits, sent forth to minister for them who shall be heirs of salvation?" *(Hebrews 1:14)*

To minister means to serve. All angels are spirit beings and have been created to serve both God and Man. Not with a *slavery* connotation, but willingly and with love.

Angels were created before Man was created. However the verse quoted above reflects the reality of foreknowledge. Angels of God were created, by God, to serve God. Because Man is a God-class creature, created *in* the image and *after* the likeness of God, angels shall serve Man as well. Angels do not serve any other angels, nor do they serve *Other Creatures* that are in a lower creation category. They minister only to God and to Man.

"For unto the angels hath he not put in subjection the world to come, whereof we speak.

But one in a certain place testified, saying, What is man, that thou are mindful of him? or the son of man, that thou visitest him?

Thou madest him a little lower than the angels (Elohim)*; thou crownest him with glory and honour, and didst set him over the works of thy hands:*

Thou has put all things in subjection under his feet. For in that he put all in subjection under him, he left nothing that is not put under him. But now we see not yet all things put under him.

But we see Jesus, . . ." *(Hebrews 2:5-9a)*

"For he hath put all things under his feet. But when he saith, All things are put under him, it is manifest that he is excepted, which did put all things under him." *(I Corinthians 15:27)*

The world to come, and all the things that have been created, are subject to the authority that God has placed within the hands of men.

At this point in time sin is still raging upon this planet, and Born-Again New Creations, for the most part, are still in infancy in utilizing their authority. But that does not change what God had done.

Currently angels are grossly under-used by the very men that they were sent forth to minister FOR. Too many times redeemed men have painted pictures of angels involved with esoteric spiritual activities. Conveying ideas that men are so far below, and much too trivial for angels to have any dealings with. When, in fact, angels are a tremendous asset for those who will recognize the truth and utilize what God has made available.

Of the myriad of activities that angels participate in, just ten of those activities found in Scripture would be:

1. Appear in dreams — *(Matthew 1:20-24)*
2. Re-gather the Nation of Israel — *(Matthew 24:31)*
3. Guard the Tree of Life — *(Genesis 3:24)*
4. Receive departed spirits — *(Luke 16:22)*
5. Influence rulership of nations — *(Daniel 10:13-21)*
6. Drive spirit horses — *(II Kings 2:12, Zechariah 1:7-11)*
7. Bring answers to prayers — *(Daniel 9:21-23)*
8. Witness confessions — *(Luke 15:8-9)*
9. Separate the good from the bad — *(Matthew 13:39-41)*
10. Help each individual — *(Matthew 18:10)*

As New Creations, we need to know what God has revealed to us, that He has made available for our stewardship.

We have the legal authority to commission angels to protect our children and property, cause that what rightfully belongs to us should find its way into our hands for the purpose of righteous stewardship, direct men and women in need of the gospel message to cross our paths, assist us in getting ourselves to the right place, and so much more. *(Hebrews 1:14)*

Angels are a valuable *tool* that God has put within our arsenal of weaponry. Let us not be derelict in utilizing them.

(9) WORDS

"Death and life are in the power of the tongue: and they that love it shall eat the fruit thereof." (Proverbs 18:21)

"But the tongue can no man tame; it is an unruly evil, full of deadly poison.
Therewith bless we God, even the Father; and therewith curse we men, which are made after the similitude of God.
Out of the same mouth proceedeth blessing and cursing. My brethren, these things ought not so to be." (James 3:8-10)

"It is the Spirit that quickeneth; the flesh profiteth nothing: the words that I speak unto you, they are spirit, and they are life." (John 6:63)

Words are spiritual seeds that we plant almost every hour of every day.

King Solomon is declaring spiritual truth realities under the inspiration of the Holy Spirit of Truth Himself. (The tongue will produce the fruit of the love of death. - or - The tongue will produce the fruit of the love of life.)

James is speaking unto carnal believers about a tongue under the influence of sin. It could be the tongue of a spiritually dead sinner, which really does not know any better . . . or it could be the tongue of a Born-Again, redeemed, New Creature who continues to give place to sin.

Jesus reveals that the words that he personally chose to speak ministered life.

Words find their origin within the primary existence realm of thought.

A word, or a series of words, is a declared and manifested thought.

The thought came first, and the word followed and conveyed the potential of that thought into being.

A word that is not spoken is not a word, it is still only a thought.

Without a spoken word, or a purposed action, a thought remains alone and powerless.

"Wherefore, my beloved brethren, let every man be swift to hear, slow to speak, slow to wrath:" (James 1:9)

"(As it is written, I have made thee a father of many nations,) before him whom he believed, even God, who quickeneth the dead, and calleth those things which be not as though they were." (Romans 4:17)

As believers, we need to pay attention to what comes out of our mouths. The Holy Spirit of God will put a check on our mouths if we will but ask Him to.

Since words are virtually creative instruments we should be sensitive to the utterances that we allow to escape our lips.

"A good man out of the good treasure of the heart bringeth forth good things: and an evil man out of the evil treasure bringeth forth evil things.

But I say unto you, That every idle word that men shall speak, they shall give account thereof in the day of judgment.

For by thy words thou shalt be justified, and by thy words thou shalt be condemned." (Matthew 12:35-37)

The "Tools" or Weaponry of Hell

"There hath no temptation taken you but such as is common to man: but God is faithful, who will not suffer (allow or permit) *you to be tempted above that ye are able; but will with the temptation also make a way of escape, that ye may be able to bear it."*
(I Corinthians 10:13)

Today we live in a world where we are continually tempted to think, and talk, and act in line with what we personally desire. God has extended His grace in protecting us from all that may be harmful unto us from within a realm that we cannot presently see with our physical eyes. Only that which is COMMON TO MAN may be used by the forces of evil to steal, kill, and destroy. *(I Corinthians 10:13)*

We have already seen that we are in a bona fide war. And we have examined the weapons or *tools* that God has provided us with to be victorious at every encounter.

However, the kingdom of darkness also has weaponry of a very deadly nature. As good stewards of eternal valuables, we need to know what those weapons or *tools* are that the devil and his agents may attempt to bring into play against us.

(1) INVALID MEMORIES OF PAST ACTIONS, ATTITUDES, THOUGHTS, WORDS, AND BELIEFS

"Therefore if any man be in Christ, he is a new creature: old things are passed away; behold, all things are become new.

And all things are of God, who hath reconciled us to himself by Jesus Christ, and hath given to us the ministry of reconciliation." (II Corinthians 5:17-18)

The Number 1 weapon that Satan utilizes against the newly created, Born-Again saints of God is Invalid Memories.

Those memories of what you once did before you were saved . . . whether just yesterday or twenty years ago, are today rendered invalid. Those memories of what you once thought in days gone by . . . are invalid. Those memories of what you once said, whether naughty or nice . . . are invalid. That medical history within your family lineage . . . is invalid. Any and all *generational curses* are invalid.

ALL **OLD THINGS ARE PASSED AWAY!** There is not one thing that potentially might be detrimental to you, coming from before you came to a saving knowledge of the Lord Jesus Christ, that has any validity whatsoever. It is __all__ passed away. It is __all__ gone. There is no record of it hiding somewhere within a file cabinet in the back room of heaven.

HOWEVER, if you personally choose to *believe* that something is still valid within your life, then you get to have whatever it is that you *believe* for, because whether you know it or not, you are exercising your faith for it.

"what things soever ye desire . . . believe that ye receive **them, and ye shall have** them. *"* *(Mark 11:24)*

Whose report will you believe . . .

Satan **counts** on us REMEMBERING all kinds of things that we know full well that we have said, or that have occurred before we received Christ Jesus, and the finished work of the cross. And he trusts us to act on, or continue to speak forth according to what we remember we once uttered or did.

That is one of the reasons that it is so imperative that we *renew our minds* on the Word of God as fast as we can. *(Romans 12:2)*

We need to disconnect ourselves from the person that we used to be . . . we need to recognize that we are now brand new in Christ Jesus.

In putting off the *"old man"* which is corrupt, and putting on the *"new man"* which is created in righteousness, we distance ourselves from all that is tainted with sin and death. *(Ephesians 4:22-24)*

Is it easy? No. But this is a war that we are in, and we had better recognize that.

And please note: This is not a war being waged over your spirit, but over your soul. Your spirit has been redeemed and recreated in Christ Jesus and is newly Born-Again. And according to the Word of God, is not able to be adversely affected by sin anymore. *(I John 3:9)* Your body is still mortal, but God has made provision for complete healing and wellness for every person that will accept it. *(Isaiah 53:5 & I Peter 2:24)* It is your soul that is on-the-line.

> *"For what shall it profit a man, if he shall gain the whole world, and lose his own soul?*
>
> *Or what shall a man give in exchange for his soul?"*
> *(Mark 8:36-37)*

The doctrine of the **saving of the soul** of man is Scripturally sound, and thousands of years old. It has been cloaked under the heading of *sanctification* in days gone by. However, it has not been boldly put forth, and extensively taught, concerning the reality of what it is that we are dealing with, within these days in which we live.

Satan cannot touch your newly Born-Again Human spirit. *(I John 3:9)* The redemption of your spirit is a work that has been done by a loving God, to a portion of your personage that you could not touch or do anything about. That is why God is the One that had to do the job. You cannot improve upon that work, and you cannot mess that work up . . . you are not the one that did it in the first place.

The entire issue at hand is the tug-of-war over your soul not your spirit. You and I have the choice of recognizing that truth and following the instructions that a loving God has given unto us that we might obtain complete victory . . . or we can deny the truth of that reality, and continue to struggle with different issues within our life that we just cannot seem to get a handle on, no matter what we do. Or we can pretend that it does not work that way, and still remain in ignorance, fulfilling the Scripture that states,

"My people are destroyed for lack of knowledge: because thou hast rejected knowledge, I will also reject thee," (Hosea 4:6)

In either case, the past is in the past and should be forgotten. Give no place for the devil to dig up anything that most assuredly is not there.

(2) CIRCUMSTANCES: WHATEVER WE MAY SEE OR HEAR

"Behold, his soul which is lifted up is not upright in him: but the just shall live by his faith." (Habakkuk 2:4)

"For therein is the righteousness of God revealed from faith to faith: as it is written, The just shall live by faith." (Romans 1:17)

"But that no man is justified by the law in the sight of God, it is evident: for, The just shall live by faith." (Galatians 3:11)

"Now the just shall live by faith: but if any man draw back, my soul shall have no pleasure in him." (Hebrews 10:38)

This author knows of no other subject pertaining to Life and godliness that the word of God has commented on, in almost exactly the same way, four different times. We really are supposed to get the message here. Faith is the foundational basis upon which everything rests.

We have personally spent decades living in a world that is defiled by sin unto the furthest reaches of every nook and cranny. And what we refer to as **_circumstances_, are the manifestation of the processes of life and death settling into the places where they have been commanded to go.** If there were no active operation of sin, there would still be circumstances in existence. However, those circumstances would always be favorable and beneficial because there would be no sin-directed command to the contrary.

"Death and life are in the power of the tongue: and they that love it shall eat the fruit thereof." (Proverbs 18:21)

"A violent man enticeth his neighbor, and leadeth him into the way that is not good.
He shutteth his eyes to devise froward things: moving his lips he bringeth evil to pass." (Proverbs 16:29-30)

The current operation of sin, on this Earth, is used by Satan to produce the circumstances that swirl around us in a tornado-like manner whether adverse or otherwise. Many times, before our new birth, we ordered our lives based upon the circumstances that presented themselves before our eyes and ears.

And since the advent of Christianity, Satan has successfully persuaded most Christians to equate the Divine Will of God to whatever might happen to *"circumstantially"* settle into place. Instead of going to the Word of God to get God's direct statement on the subject, Christians will just declare that *"God is in control"*, and whatsoever circumstantially occurs must have some good reason behind it, and so it must be God's will. And the Word of God, which states, *"My people are destroyed for lack of knowledge"* (Hosea 4:6) finds its fulfillment again and again and again. My brethren, these things ought not so to be.

It is true that individually, we must purpose to be aware of what is happening all around us. However, to simply passively accept the natural and ignore the Scripturally declared super-natural is not wise. We again, need to purpose to become more and more familiar with what the Word of God declares is indeed reality, and then choose to agree with life, godliness, and victory. We then need to audibly declare what our God has said is so, that we might set into motion words of power, from lips of authority, that are able to alter and change the *circumstances* around us to line up with truth.

(3) FEARS OF: NOT GOOD ENOUGH, NOTHING TO SAY OR CONTRIBUTE, NO TALENT, REJECTION, I DO NOT KNOW HOW TO DO IT, I CANNOT DO IT, ETC.

"For God hath not given us the spirit of fear; but of power, and of love, and of a sound mind." (II Timothy 1:7)

The Spirit of Fear is one of the fifteen named, active *Strongmen* spirits currently operating within the kingdom of darkness on this planet Earth. It is part of the *"principalities and powers"* (Ephesians 6:12) that we wrestle against. Jesus said,

"No man can enter into a strong man's house, and spoil his goods, except he will first bind the strong man; and then he will spoil his house." (Mark 3:27)

For someone who does not know the Lord Jesus Christ as their personal savior, fear can be a terrifying, driving force and able to paralyze that person from being able to speak or to act. Fear is real and powerful, and the devil knows how to use it.

However, any person who is a New Creation *in Christ* has been swept totally clean on the inside, and the application of the blood of Jesus Christ has purged us of all Sin, and made all things new. And because we are *in Christ*, and seated with him at the right hand of our Father in heaven, we are now the *boss* in any given situation and are the ones in charge. We do not have to allow ourselves to be intimidated by the threats coming from the powers of darkness any longer.

Fear comes from the outside of a Born-Again Christian and knocks on the door to try and get you to let it back in again. You may be tempted to once again fear something or someone, however, the *"quick and powerful, sharper than any two-edged sword"* (Hebrews 4:12) Word

43

of God tells us that *"I can do all things through Christ which strengtheneth me."* *(Philippians 4:13)*

Fear does not come from God. In fact,

"There is no fear in love; but perfect love casteth out fear: because fear hath torment. He that feareth is not made perfect in love." *(I John 4:18)*

That is not to say that because a person is *in Christ* they will not ever be tempted to fear again. That temptation is frightfully real. But the choice as to whether or not to yield to that temptation is still left up to each and every one of us. And yet reality states: *"I can do all things through Christ which strengtheneth me"* *(Philippians 4:13)* and *"if God be for us, who can be against us".* *(Romans 8:31)* We do not have to give in to that temptation.

Does it take courage to stand-up against fear? Yes, it does. Does it take courage to speak out or do something that you have never done before? Yes, it does. Will the Lord help us if we choose to move and act in faith? Yes, He will.

We are New Creations. Brand new. I am not simply a re-model of the same old me. *"Old things are passed away,"* and *"all things are become new."* *(II Corinthians 5:17)* So I need to gird up my loins, and with my faith step out, and trust in the Lord to see me through any given situation.

(4) EMOTIONS

"Who shall ascend into the hill of the Lord? or who shall stand in his holy place?

He that hath clean hands, and a pure heart; who hath not lifted up his soul unto vanity, nor sworn deceitfully." *(Psalm 24:3-4)*

"A man of great wrath shall suffer punishment: for if thou deliver him, yet thou must do it again." (Proverbs 19:19)

"Wrath is cruel, and anger is outrageous; but who is able to stand before envy?" (Proverbs 27:4)

"Surely the churning of milk bringeth forth butter, and the wringing of the nose bringeth forth blood: so the forcing of wrath bringeth forth strife." (Proverbs 30:33)

Emotions are a major component of the soul within every Man or Woman. They have been originally designed and ordained by God for the benefits that come with the gift of *Life*. They are supposed to be a benefit and a blessing. However, they were not originally created by God, to lead or to govern an individual.

The spirit of the Man is the core-portion of the individual that was divinely designed to shoulder the weight of responsibility and to make all of the necessary decisions.

The soul of the Man, which includes the emotional component, was designed only to assist the spirit of the individual, and facilitate the necessary operations that occur between the spirit portion and the body of that person.

And the body of any person, which is the housing for the spirit and the soul of an individual to dwell within, was designed by God to do whatever it is ordered to do by either the spirit or the assiting soul.

When the core-spirit of the species called Man spiritually died with Adam's disobedience and Sin, the assisting soul of Adam, and the assisting soul of all of the other Human Beings that have emanated forth from him was automatically, involuntarily, thrust into the leadership position that the spirit should occupy, and according to the word of God the creature called Man *"became a living soul"*. (Genesis 2:7b)

Emotions can be extremely volatile. Emotions can erupt into volcanic consequences at a moment's notice. The devil, and all of *Hell*, revels in the fact that the souls of all men are currently in the leadership position . . . and have been in that position since the death of all men's spirits. Satan has been able to successfully utilized the emotional portion of the soul of men as a weapon or tool against all of Mankind and all of that which God has called His Man to do.

In order for the soul of a man to find its proper place once again, and operate as God originally designed it to, a man must become Born-Again within his core-spirit. The spiritually dead spirit of a man must receive New Life, which has become available from the finished work of Jesus Christ of Nazareth upon the cross of Calvary. Once that occurs the spirit of that same man must be nourished and strengthened, and encouraged to grow to the extent that it is able to subdue the assisting soul that has been running amok since that individual was born into this world.

As long as a man's assisting soul is allowed to remain in charge of his being, whether that individual is Born-Again or not, the emotional part of that man's soul remains subject to being an extraordinarily real, and viable weapon of *Hell*.

(5) PHYSICAL HANDICAPS

"He is despised and rejected of men; a man of sorrows, and acquainted with grief: and we hid as it were out faces from him; he was despised, and we esteemed him not.

Surely he hath borne our griefs, and carried our sorrows: yet we did esteem him stricken, smitten of God, and afflicted.

But he was wounded for our transgressions, he was bruised for our iniquities: the chastisement of our peace was upon him; and with his stripes we are healed." (Isaiah 53:3-5)

"Who his own self bare our sins in his own body on the tree, that we, being dead to sins, should live unto righteousness: by whose stripes ye were healed." (I Peter 2:24)

Many, many times the Satanic weapon of physical handicaps is just too sensitive of an issue to bring up and onto the table. If we seriously look at the physical suffering of others as being an active weapon of the kingdom of darkness, it is all too often perceived that we demonstrate our callousness and hardness of heart.

So, rather than recognize the actual truth of the matter, we willingly move over into the soulish arena of emotions . . . and empathy and pity become the order of the day.

Ladies and gentlemen, we are in a real WAR, and we had better recognize the truth of that, much sooner than later. The enemy comes for no other reason, *"but for to steal, and to kill, and to destroy:"* *(John 10:10)* and physical handicaps that Satan is able to strap onto unsuspecting people do just that. Do not expect any of the agents from the kingdom of darkness to *play fair.*

Even the secular world of men dead in their sins understands that you cannot have your cake and eat it too. Either God *"sent his word, and healed them, and delivered* them *from their destructions"* *(Psalm 107:20)* or He did not . . . which is it? Either *"he was wounded for our transgressions,* (and) *he was bruised for our iniquities:* (and) *the chastisement of our peace was upon him; and with his stripes we are healed."* *(Isaiah 53:5)* or we are not . . . which is it? And the limp-wristed 'Well, you know, God doesn't heal everybody!' is declared Scriptural ignorance, and does not wash when you put it up against the declared truth. *(John 17:17)* So . . . once again, who's report will we believe?

Is it going to be an easy thing to stand upon the Word of God in the face of so much circumstantial and contradictory evidence? No, not necessarily. Would we like it to be easy? Of course we would. Would we like everything that is of a super-natural foundation, and operating within a realm that we cannot see into with our naked eyes, to be easy? Of course we would. Sadly, it is not going to operate that way. And we must Scripturally *". . . take it by force"* *(Matthew 11:12)*

However, by the grace of God, we do have the Creator of all things on our side. And, we have God's unchanging word. And, we have the faithfulness of God's promise. And, we have the dynamics of God's power. And, we have the Holy Spirit of God living within us. So, the victory in any given situation, should always be ours. And so if at the first application of our faith we do not succeed, we need to continue to try, try, again.

Physical handicaps present a towering mountain of physical and spiritual difficulty to overcome. Aside from the miraculous intervening hand of God in a given situation, a person with a physical handicap needs to become personally, spiritually mature, in order to obtain the desired victory. There is no margin for error in dealing with something that is so physically overwhelming and obvious. There are no half-way measures that will succeed. It will either be victory or defeat . . . success or failure . . . healed or infirmed. This is spiritual reality and serious stuff that we are involved with here. There are no handicapped people living anywhere in heaven. And, the position of "It's just too hard" or "I just can't do it" are not accepted statements within the halls of reality and truth. The declared Word of God, that was sent forth to heal them is, in the final reality, the bottom line.

(6) PEOPLE
BOTH SAVED AND UNSAVED

"The Lord hath made all things for himself: yea, even the wicked for the day of evil." (Proverbs 16:4)

"Again, When a righteous man doth turn from his righteousness, and commit iniquity, and I lay a stumblingblock before him, he shall die: because thou hast not given him warning, he shall die in his sin, and his righteousness which he hath done shall not be remembered; but his blood will I require at thine hand." (Ezekiel 3:20)

The operating parameter of the whole Humanity program that we are involved with while we are on this earth is Life and Death; Blessing and Cursing; Success and Failure; Victory and Defeat; White and Black. And, there is no gray area to be found within the entire scenario.

People are people. And people will continue to do what people will continue to do. So the question becomes, who is the one that is invisibly directing these people to do what it is that they do?

The *"wicked man"* is not *wicked* right from his bassinet. He begins his life no differently than a righteousness man. Somewhere along the way during his early years he learns what the difference is between that which is right and correct, and that which is wrong and not correct. And he ultimately chooses the direction that he <u>wants</u> to go in.

"There is a way which seemeth right unto a man; but the end thereof are the ways of death." (Proverbs 14:12 & Proverbs 16:25)

From all over the planet, every single individual who is not **Born-Again**, legally belongs to the prince of the power of the air, and is a citizen of his kingdom of darkness. And each one of those individuals is potentially an active agent for service in the realm of death and destruction, even if on the surface they appear to be a very *nice person*.

They are in a condition of being spiritually dead in their sins. They are currently captives to the Law of Sin and its power to compel men in *"for what I would, that do I not — but what I hate, that do I."* (Romans 7:15)

Their personal inclination may not necessarily be that **"every imagination of the thoughts of their hearts was only evil continually",** (Genesis 6:5) but they think in a two-dimensional manner and not normally in line with what the Word of God declares.

Their mouths may not be fully inclined to line up with *"moving his lips he bringeth evil to pass"* (Proverbs 16:30) at all times, but they do not usually speak forth words of truth filled with life.

Their actions may not be fully reprobate, and in line with '*the man who bringeth wicked devices to pass'* (Psalms 37:7), but most of what they will actually do will fall in line with the prevailing circumstances, the lusts of the flesh, and the reactions that will occur to whatsoever it is that they might encounter.

They are literally pawns in an invisible game of life and death chess and are not even aware of it. If the invisible veil that separates the two worlds were to be lifted and an opportunity afforded to peer into the spiritual realm they would be shockingly surprised to see how many *strings* are actually attached to their free-will. They are fully _ententacled_ to this natural realm, and captives to their fives physical senses.

For the most part, they genuinely do not purpose to be *wicked* people; however, that is just the way that life works.

As a notation, a large percentage of New Creation individuals who have been *"delivered from the power of darkness, and translated into the kingdom of his dear Son"* (Colossians 1:13) are almost just as actively involved in wickedness as those who remain in legal captivity.

As children of light, we have been commanded to *"renew our minds",* (Romans 12:2) and to *"put on the mind of Christ"* (Romans 13:14) and change the way that we think. But is that what usually happens?

As sons and daughters of God we have been commanded to be *"quick to hear, slow to speak, and slow to wrath"* (James 1:19) and to *"speak not evil one of another"* (James 4:11) and to let our *"yea be yea; and our nay, nay."* (James 5:12) But is that what usually happens?

As agents of righteousness, we have been commanded to be *"doers of the word, and not hearers only, deceiving our own selves"* (James 1:22) and to *"cleanse ourselves of all filthiness of the flesh and spirit, perfecting holiness in the fear of God."* (II Corinthians 7:1) But is that what usually happens?

Like natural seeds in the hands of a farmer, Sin continues to be sown into this earth one idle or wicked word at a time; one reprobate or renegade thought at a time; one irreverent or inappropriate action at a time. And, *Hell* is delighted to use whatever spiritually ignorant, independent agent, that there may be, who would be willing to do the bidding of the prince of darkness.

Being *in Christ* does not exempt us from being used by the devil. We, ourselves, are the determining factor. The decisions are ours to make. I cannot decide for you, nor judge you in what you decide. And you cannot decide for me, nor judge me in what I decide. This is a one-on-one continual encounter with the word of truth and the Spirit of Grace.

What we can do, on a positive note, is exhort one another. What we can do is pledge ourselves to become accountable to another brother or sister in Christ. To willingly allow someone to *hold our feet to fire* as it were, as far as what we say and what we do where our personal behavior is concerned.

It does not take rocket science to understand that if we leave things the way that they are, Sin will continue to be victorious. Without any changes, there will be no change.

May the mercy and the prevailing grace of God continue to stretch a covering of protection over us in these last days in which we live.

(7) WORDS

"Death and life are in the power of the tongue: and they that love it shall eat the fruit thereof." (Proverbs 18:21)

"A hypocrite with his *mouth destroyeth his neighbor: but through knowledge shall the just be delivered."* (Proverbs 11:9)

"The wicked is snared by the transgression of his *lips: but the just shall come out of trouble."* (Proverbs 12:13)

"An ungodly man diggeth up evil: and in his lips there is *as a burning fire."* (Proverbs 16:27)

The Book of Proverbs is profuse with statements concerning the tongue and the power that is contained within the words that we speak.

Just as with the *"Weapons of our Warfare"* (II Corinthians 10:4) of the believer, so it is with the dominion of darkness and the *tools* that they use. Words are spiritual seeds that we plant almost every hour of every day.

For the most part, small children do not know what the word of God declares. *(Which is why we are told to raise up a child in the way that they should go, and when they are old they will not depart from it.)*

But small children do listen to what comes out of their parents mouths. Children cultivate vocabulary from what they hear at home from mom and dad, what they hear from the friends of mom and dad, what they hear on the television, what they hear in movies, what their school friends say, and so many other unnamed sources.

People normally *react* to any given situation, they do not *respond*. When they react, the mouth is usually engaged at full throttle. Words begin to pour out of lips of authority that cannot be brought back or recovered. Negative words create negative things. Vile words create vile things. Angry words create angry things.

And even though these *bad* things will not come about right away, they **will** come into existence as they are gathered together and the universal laws that control creativity and how things work grab hold of them and begin to mold and shape them into the very substance that the words have declared.

May the Lord of grace help us to curb our tongue.

Spiritual Warfare

"Lest Satan should get an advantage of us: for we are not ignorant of his devices." (II Corinthians 2:11)

We have looked in detail within Chapter 1 of this study, at the **"Armour of God"** (Ephesians 6:11) that is spoken of by the Apostle Paul in his letter to the Ephesians, and that has been made available by our God for us to use.

And we have observed and ascertained just how to utilize each piece of that armour for our maximum benefit.

We have looked in detail within Chapter 2 of this study, at the nine *"Weapons of our Warfare"* (IICorinthians 10:4) that are spoken of by the Apostle Paul in his second letter to the Corinthians. And we have studied the Scriptural validity of those weapons, and discussed just how we might utilize them to the best of our ability.

We have looked in detail within Chapter 3 of this study, at seven different devices of Satan that we have labeled as **"Weapons of Hell"** that the prince of the power of the air utilizes against the saints of God to the best of his defiled ability, or the ability of his *company toadies* - agents of darkness.

We shall conclude our study with six Scriptural examples of actual warfare situations, and the weapons that were involved within these situations, and the ultimate outcome of each of the skirmishes. And finally, with ten *"where the rubber-meets-the-road"* real 21st century scenarios that we, as believers, face on a day to day basis.

(1) SODOM AND GOMORRAH

"But before they lay down, the men of the city, even the men of Sodom, compassed the house round, both old and young, all the people from every quarter:

And they called unto Lot, and said unto him, Where are the men which came in to thee this night? bring them out unto us, that we may know them.

And Lot went out at the door unto them, and shut the door after him.

And said, I pray you, brethren, do not so wickedly." (*Genesis 19:4-7*)

"*And they said, Stand back. And they said again, This one fellow came in to sojourn, and he will needs be a judge: now will we deal worse with thee than with them. And they pressed sore upon the man, even Lot, and came near to break the door.*

But the men put forth their hand and pulled Lot into the house to them, and shut to the door.

And they smote the men that were at the door of the house with blindness, both small and great: so that they wearied themselves to find the door." (*Genesis 19:9-11*)

"*And when the morning arose, then the angels hastened Lot, saying, Arise, take thy wife, and thy two daughters, which are here; least thou be consumed in the iniquity of the city.*

And while he lingered, the men laid hold upon his hand, and upon the hand of his wife, and upon the hand of his two daughters; the Lord being merciful unto him: and they brought him forth, and set him without the city.

And it came to pass, when they had brought them forth abroad, that he said, Escape for thy life; look not behind thee, neither stay thou in all the plain; escape to the mountain, lest thou be consumed.

And Lot said unto them, Oh, not so, my Lord:

Behold now, thy servant hath found grace in thy sight, and thou hast magnified thy mercy, which thou hast shown unto me in saving my life; and I cannot escape to the mountain, lest some evil take me, and I die:

Behold now, this city is near to flee unto, and it is a little one: O, let me escape thither, (is it not a little one?) and my soul shall live.

And he said unto him, See, I have accepted thee concerning this thing also, that I will not overthrow this city, for the which thou hast spoken.

Haste thee, escape thither; for I cannot do anything till thou be come thither. Therefore the name of the city was called Zoar.

The sun was risen upon the earth when Lot entered into Zoar.

Then the Lord rained upon Sodom and upon Gomorrah brimstone and fire from the Lord out of heaven;

And he overthrew those cities, and all the plain, and all the inhabitants of the cities, and that which grew upon the ground.

But his wife looked back from behind him, and she became a pillar of salt." (Genesis 19:15-26)

"And it came to pass, when God destroyed the cities of the plain, that God remembered Abraham, and sent Lot out of the midst of the overthrow, when he overthrew the cities in the which Lot dwelt.

And Lot went up out of Zoar, and dwelt in the mountain, and his two daughters with him; for he feared to dwell in Zoar: and he dwelt in a cave, he and his two daughters." (Genesis 19:29-30)

What is the given situation here in Genesis within our first example?

A man who is considered righteous *(II Peter 2:7-8)* in the eyes of God is in danger of being harmed by reprobate men totally given over unto the powers of darkness.

What *"Armour of God"* may be potentially available for use at this point?

Even though, the specific *"Armour of God"* is not Scripturally laid out before Abraham, he is *"girding his loins with truth"* in his querying of God Himself . . .

"And Abraham drew near, and said, Wilt thou destroy the righteous with the wicked?" (Genesis 18:23)

"That be far from thee to do after this manner, to slay the righteous with the wicked: and that the righteous should be as the wicked, that be far from thee: Shall not the Judge of all the earth do right?" (Genesis 18:25)

What *"Weapons of Hell"* are then employed by the kingdom of darkness and being brought to bear against Abraham's nephew Lot in this given situation?

(1) Circumstances - Biblically speaking, a man of light was dwelling within a cesspool of darkness. And it is true that he was dwelling there by his own choice. Even so, were the circumstances of the condition of the city of Sodom unfavorable toward Lot? Yes, they were. Could Lot honestly have done anything to change those unfavorable circumstance? No, not at this late date. Was Lot allowing himself to be affected by those circumstances? Yes, he was.

(2) Fears - Wicked men lusted to impose themselves upon righteous 'men', and Lot was perceived to be a barrier to that imposition. Was Lot being pressed upon to give in to sinful and evil actions in Sodom? Yes, he was. Did Lot succumb to fear because of those threats? Yes, he did. After Lot was delivered from the city of Sodom, was he afraid to escape into the mountains as he was directed? Yes, he was. When God spared the little city of Zoar because of Lot's petition, which was based upon fear, was Lot then afraid to dwell in Zoar, so ultimately he came and dwelt in the mountains anyway? Yes, he was.

(3) Emotions - Lustful emotions, on a regular basis, raged within the inhabitants of the city of Sodom as part of their life-style. Emotions of anger and indignation erupted when the citizens were prohibited from 'having their way' with the righteous visitors. Did these emotional outbursts pose a danger to Lot? Yes, they did. Was Lot able to quell their emotions through reason? No, he was not. Did these unchecked emotions lead these individuals to unrighteous actions? Yes, they did.

(4) People - The whole of the citizenry of the city of Sodom were active agents of hell, even if they were not aware of it. The established reputation of the city testifies of a conscious, knowing, willing departure from that which is known to be right and true. Within Sodom was Lot being imposed upon and threatened by these wicked people? Yes, he was. Were these people intent upon harming Lot because he would not yield to their lusts? Yes, they were.

(5) Words - Conversation occurred between the citizens of the city and Lot when the strangers arrived. Lot attempted to deal with a volatile situation through reason, even to a point of moral compromise with members of his own family. Were words spoken to Lot in order to gender the fear and intimidation that was being imposed upon him? Yes, they were. Did those words ultimately have an effect upon Lot's actions? Yes, they did.

Lot is a man who is living in a natural visible world, but he is being assaulted by forces from the invisible super-natural realm, utilizing the weaponry that has a direct connection with the natural visible world. Light is under attack by darkness. The intent is to ***"steal, kill, and destroy"*** *(John 10:10)* the light so that the darkness may prevail. It is a real spiritual battle, within a real spiritual war.

Was Lot a man who was in a covenant relationship with the Living God? No, but Abraham was.

Did Lot himself ask for help from either God or Abraham? No, he did not, but Abraham knew that he was going to need some help because he knew where Lot lived and the recently pronounced judgment that had come from God upon the city and its inhabitants.

Was Lot adversely affected by the circumstances that swirled all around him? Yes, he was. Did Lot succumb to various fears that presented themselves? Yes, he did. Did emotions become enraged when lust was not allowed to run its course? Yes, they did. Was Lot being imposed upon and threatened by wicked people? Yes, he was. Were words spoken to Lot to gender fear and intimidation? Yes, they were.

What *"Weapons of our Warfare"*, within this first example, do we see might be available and able to be employed during this scenario?

(1) Prayer - of an intercessory nature, by a covenant man, on behalf of other righteous men or women. *(Genesis 18:23-33)(James 5:16b)*

(2) Holy Angels - commissioned by God to minister for those who would be the heirs of salvation. *(Hebrews 1:14)* Sent to physically deliver recipients of mercy from destruction and death.

Did the effectual fervent prayer of a righteous man avail much in this particular instance? Yes, it did.

Were holy angels dispatched in a timely manner to minister for those who would be the heirs of salvation? Yes, they were.

Who ultimately prevailed and enjoyed the victory within this situation—the kingdom of Light or the kingdom of Darkness?

Did this deliverance from God personally affect Lot's life in a positive manner? No, it did not. Lot still continued to be fearful, and his inappropriate behavior is cataloged as an example for us to learn from. However, righteousness did prevail over unrighteousness, as it is possible for anyone who is in a covenant relationship with the Living God to do every single time.

(2) DANIEL AND THE LION'S DEN

"Then this Daniel was preferred above the presidents and princes, because an excellent spirit was in him; and the king thought to set him over the whole realm.

Then the presidents and princes sought to find occasion against Daniel concerning the kingdom; but they could find none occasion nor fault; forasmuch as he was faithful, neither was there any error or fault found in him.

Then said these men, We shall not find any occasion against this Daniel, except we find it against him concerning the law of his God.

Then these presidents and princes assembled together to the king, and said thus unto him, King Darius, live for ever.

All the presidents of the kingdom, the governors, and the princes, the counsellors, and the captains, have consulted together to establish a royal statute, and to make a firm decree, that whosoever shall ask a petition of any God or man for thirty days, save of thee, O king, he shall be cast into the den of lions.

Now, O king, establish the decree, and sign the writing, that it be not changed, according to the law of the Medes and Persians, which altereth not.

Wherefore King Darius signed the writing and the decree.

Now when Daniel knew that the writing was signed, he went into his house; and his windows being open in his chamber toward Jerusalem, he kneeled upon his knees three times a day, and prayed, and gave thanks before his God, as he did aforetime.

Then these men assembled, and found Daniel praying and making supplication before his God.

Then they came near, and spake before the king concerning the king's decree; Hast thou not signed a decree, that every man that shall ask a petition of any God or man within thirty days, save of thee, O king, shall be cast into the den of lions? The king *answered and said, The thing is true, according to the law of the Medes and Persians, which altereth not.*

Then answered they and said before the king, That Daniel, which is of the children of the captivity of Judah, regardeth not thee, O king, nor the decree that thou hast signed, but maketh his petition three times a day.

Then the king, when he heard these words, was sore displeased with himself, and set his heart on Daniel to deliver him: and he laboured till the going down of the sun to deliver him.

Then these men assembled unto the king, and said unto the king, Know, O king, that the law of the Medes and Persians is, That no decree nor statute which the king establisheth may be changed.

Then the king commanded, and they brought Daniel, and cast him into the den of lions. Now the king spake and said unto Daniel, Thy God whom thou servest continually, he will deliver thee.

And a stone was brought, and laid upon the mouth of the den; and the king sealed it with his own signet, and with the signet of his lords; that the purpose might not be changed concerning Daniel.

Then the king went to his palace, and passed the night fasting: neither were instruments of music brought before him: and his sleep went from him.

Then the king arose very early in the morning, and went in haste unto the den of lions.

And when he came to the den, he cried with a lamentable voice unto Daniel: and the king spake and said to Daniel, O Daniel, servant of the living God, is thy God, whom thou servest continually, able to deliver thee from the lions?

Then said Daniel unto the king, O king, live for ever.

My God hath sent his angel, and hath shut the lion's mouths, that they have not hurt me: forasmuch as before him innocency was found in me; and also before thee, O king, have I done no hurt.

Then was the king exceeding glad for him, and commanded that they should take Daniel up out of the den, and no manner of hurt was found upon him, because he believed in his God.

And the king commanded, and they brought those men which had accused Daniel, and they cast them *into the den of lions, them, their children, and their wives; and the lions had the mastery of them, and brake all their bones in pieces or ever they came at the bottom of the den."* (Daniel 6:3-24)

What is the situation that we have here in this second example?

A covenant man with an *"excellent spirit"* (Daniel 5:12) was verbally attacked by jealous and envious agents of darkness that were bent on destroying him.

Again, even though at this point the *"Armour of God"* is not specifically, Scripturally laid out before him, Daniel is an Abrahamic Covenant man, walking in the light of the Law of Moses.

And he is actually donning the *Breastplate of Righteousness* by actively walking in the light of God's word and by choosing to obey God's instructions in all things.

He is taking up the *Shield of Faith* by placing his trust in, and believing, what God has said is so . . . in spite of what other evidence may be presenting itself. So, the Holy Spirit of protection is on the job.

What *"Weapons of Hell"* were being brought to bare against Daniel by the unwitting agents of the kingdom of darkness?

(1) Circumstances - Daniel is a godly man living in captivity, who has conducted himself righteously and thus has received favor from the current ruling authorities. Were the circumstances that produced jealousy and envy, against that given favor, within his political captivity, advantageous for Daniel? No, they were not.

(2)   Fears - Jealousy is a by-product of fear. Jealous men were fearful that Daniel would continue to increase in influencing men in authority, and in so doing would possibly jeopardize their positions and future. Was Daniel in any real danger because of these jealous men? Yes, he was. Was Daniel's own death a distinct possibility within this Lion's Den scenario? Yes, it was.

Is it also possible that Daniel was tempted to be worried or concerned for his own safety? Yes, it certainly was.

(3)   Emotions - Envy, jealousy, contempt, and anger, were just a sample of the emotions that may have been stirred within these individuals. These unrighteous emotions, left unchecked, would drive them to their ultimate actions of destruction and death. Overpowering normal intelligence and common sense for the sake of wicked satisfaction.

(4) People - Unrighteous men with personal agendas are able to be used as pawns by Satan against a righteous man in covenant with the Living God. Were these jealous men in any position to present a substantial threat to Daniel? Yes, they were. Was their focused intention to destroy Daniel if at all possible? Yes, it was. Did they know that they were being successfully used by the powers of darkness? No, probably not.

(5)   Words – Specifically chosen words were spoken to the king by jealous men who were fearful that their position and their influence was in jeopardy. Were these words subtly spoken to the king for the purpose of setting a snare for Daniel? Yes, they were. Was the king, who was favorable toward Daniel, displeased with himself when he had heard that certain words he had spoken were used against him? Yes, he was, upon reflection of those words.

Do we see any Scriptural evidence of Daniel being worried or concerned at the charges that are brought against him? No, we do not, at least not Scripturally. Would any worry or concern have helped

Daniel? Or really done any good to change the outcome of the situation? No, it would not.

Spiritual warfare usually involves individuals of righteousness defending themselves against the assaults launched by various agents within the kingdom of darkness. It is the *standard operating procedure* of Satan and the company toadies of his kingdom to attempt to steal from, or to kill, or to destroy men and women of righteousness.

Again, within the Book of Daniel we have a recorded incident of the kingdom of darkness, using willing Human agents, to launch a death assault against a covenant individual within the kingdom of light.

What **"Weapons of our Warfare"** might be able to be observed within this scenario?

(1) Faith - Daniel choosing to place his trust in, and believe, what God has stated within His word, in spite of what other evidence may present itself to the contrary. *(Psalm 119:89)*

(2) Prayer - Daniel's potential prayer of a deliverance nature, by a covenant man who was aware of the trap of wickedness that had been set against him, concerning his commitment to his God. *(Daniel 6:10)*

(3) Holy Angels - ministering for those who would be heirs of salvation. *(Daniel 16:22)(Hebrews 1:14)* Angels were commissioned, and indeed intervened and caused the mouths of the hungry lions to remain closed toward Daniel.

Did the effectual fervent prayer of a righteous man avail much in this instance? Yes, it did, as it always does.

Were holy angels dispatched to minister for those who would be heirs of salvation? Yes, they were.

We see that Daniel is a man who knows the God whom he serves. His fellowship with his God is more than just casual. And because God is a faithful covenant-keeping God, deliverance is once again the final outcome of this incident.

But that deliverance is not automatic. Even though prayer has been set forth, Daniel has a part to play as well and must take a stand against the unrighteousness that presents itself as victorious. Daniel must exercise *"and having done all, to stand."* (Ephesians 6:13) faith.

In spiritual warfare — whether concerning that which has already occurred in days gone by, or that which is occurring presently — we must understand that there are two sides of the coin. God has His part to play, and that is side one. And we have our part to play and that is side two. We must choose to be doers of the word and not hearers only (James 1:22). We can be assured that God will always do His part because of His faithfulness. The question ultimately becomes will we diligently do our part?

(3) THE TEMPTATION IN THE WILDERNESS

"Then was Jesus led up of the Spirit into the wilderness to be tempted of the devil.

And when he had fasted forty days and forty nights, he was afterward an hungered.

And when the tempter came to him, he said, If thou be the Son of God, command that these stones be made bread.

But he answered and said, It is written, Man shall not live by bread alone, but by every word that proceedeth out of the mouth of God.

Then the devil taketh him up into the holy city, and setteth him on a pinnacle of the temple.,

And saith unto him, If thou be the Son of God, cast thyself down: for it is written, He shall give his angels charge concerning thee: and in their hands they shall bear thee up, lest at any time thou dash thy foot against a stone.

Jesus said unto him, It is written again, Thou shalt not tempt the Lord thy God.

Again, the devil taketh him up into an exceeding high mountain, and showeth him all the kingdoms of the world, and the glory of them;

And saith unto him, All these things will I give thee, if thou wilt fall down and worship me.

Then saith Jesus unto him, Get thee hence, Satan: for it is written, Thou shalt worship the Lord thy God, and him only shalt thou serve.

Then the devil leaveth him, and, behold, angels came and ministered unto him." (Matthew 4:1-11)

What is the situation here within the gospel accounts, concerning the perfect Human Being himself?

A sinless covenant man, with an assignment from God to repair the breach that the Law of Sin has caused, is being challenged to fall prey to temptation and transgress against the truth.

Even though, Jesus of Nazareth is the word of God manifest in the flesh, he must put on the full *"Armour of God"* just like any other man.

(1) Belt of Truth - Jesus knows what the truth is and he is speaking the truth at every opportunity.

(2) Breastplate of Righteousness - Jesus is actively walking in the light of God's word, and choosing to obey His instructions in all things.

(3) Preparation of the Gospel of Peace - Jesus knows who he is and is always ready to impart words that gender hope to every man or woman that he may meet.

(4) Shield of Faith - Jesus is choosing to place his trust in, and believe, what God has stated is so . . . in spite of what other evidence may present itself.

(5) Helmet of Salvation - Jesus knows in mind and heart what the Holy Spirit has revealed unto him, concerning who he is. And he is walking in that confidence.

What *"Weapons of Hell"* were being employed by Satan with this assault?

(1) Invalid Memories - Twice the devil invisibly whispers in Jesus' ear "IF thou be the Son of God . . ." attempting to challenge him to believe that he is just a regular man. And indeed, if he is more than just a regular man then he needs to prove, at the very least to himself, his Divinity that the Holy Spirit revealed unto him when he was twelve, and thus perform a miracle.

(2) Circumstances - Jesus has fasted for forty days, and he is hungry, and there is no one around to witness what he might do, so it might be time to turn a stone into bread and eat.

(3) Fears - The thoughts that are presented to him are . . . "are you really who you think you are?", then you need to prove it just to make sure. "What if you decide to do something, and it does not work? What will people say then?"

(4) Emotions - Jesus of Nazareth has emotions just like everyone else. And the Scriptures reveal that he was *"despised and rejected of men"*. *(Isaiah 53:3)* This author believes that the rejection that is being spoken of was not just something that began with the on-set of his public ministry. Then, there is the very real potential of the loneliness of being in the wilderness with only the company of rocks and reptiles to surround you. Sadness at the thought of Man's rebellion and departure from the glory and blessings that God had originally planned for him. And other real emotions that were going to have to be dealt with victoriously.

(5) Words - Satan did not visibly appear to Jesus in the wilderness as Hollywood so often portrays it. There was no other 'person' around at the time, and Jesus was quite alone. Although Scripturally speaking spoken words were not used, nevertheless the intensely real words that might have become the product of suggested thoughts, were utilized by Satan to apply tremendous pressure to Jesus' free-will.

What *"Weapons of our Warfare"* are seen as being active in this example of assault against Jesus?

(1) The Word of God - In dealing with the invisible Devil, Jesus speaks seemingly into the air when he says, *"It is written . . ."* against all three of the recorded temptations. Even though there is no visible *person* around, the word of God is *"quick and powerful"* and *"shall not return unto me void, but it shall accomplish that which I please."* In speaking the word aloud, Jesus is putting God in remembrance of His word, *(Isaiah 43:26)* nullifying the opportunities of temptation, *(II Corinthians 10:5)* rebuking the Devil, *(James 4:7)* and reminding himself as a man of the faithfulness of what his God has declared, all at the same time.

(2) Faith - As a man, Jesus has placed his trust in, and believed, what God has stated is so . . . in spite of what other evidence may present itself. Now, with each declaration of *"It is written . . ."* Jesus releases his faith in the ability of God's word to produce results. *(Isaiah 55:11)*

(3) Holy Spirit power - Jesus has recently become cloaked with the Holy Spirit of God. Jesus *boldly* takes a stand against temptation, receives the words that the Spirit of Truth brings to his attention, *remembers* what the Holy Spirit revealed unto him at a young age, operates in discernment of where these thoughts are coming from, and slams the door on Satan.

(4) Words - Jesus is speaking under the unction of the Holy Spirit of God. What he utters is succinct and to the point. He has chosen life and speaks words perfectly in line with that which he has chosen to believe.

(5) Holy Angels - At the conclusion of the spiritual combat, holy angels of God came and ministered comfort unto Jesus, and the peace of God flooded his being.

Many people think that because Jesus of Nazareth was God manifest in the flesh that he did not have any real difficulties with the Devil because, after all, when it comes right down to it, he is God. And if the Devil does not watch out concerning what he is doing, Jesus will just 'POOF' him out of existence. It does not quite work that way at all.

In becoming a Man, Jesus is going to be just like his brethren in every respect. Whatever frailties or short-comings there may be with becoming a Human Being, Jesus is going to have them. Men, finding themselves in a spiritual war, have to read and to study the Word of God . . . and so did Jesus. Men, if they choose to, have to commit to memory the Word of God . . . and so did Jesus. Men have to submit themselves therefore unto God and resist the devil . . . and so did Jesus.

As a man Jesus of Nazareth had a free-will and the same opportunity as all other men to yield to temptation and sin. If the truth is that he did not genuinely have that opportunity to fail . . . then he is not the **"last Adam,"** *(I Corinthians 15:45)* and he had an unfair advantage because of his being God, and what he secured for Mankind is not legal and just.

(4) JESUS WITHIN THE CITY OF NAZARETH

"And he came to Nazareth, where he had been brought up: and, as his custom was, he went into the synagogue on the sabbath day, and stood up for to read.

And there was delivered unto him the book of the prophet Isaiah. And when he had opened the book, he found the place where it was written,

The Spirit of the Lord is upon me, because he hath anointed me to preach to gospel to the poor; he hath sent me to heal the broken-hearted, to preach deliverance to the captives, and recovering of sight to the blind, to set at liberty them that are bruised,

To preach the acceptable year of the Lord.

And he closed the book, and he gave it again to the minister, and sat down. And the eyes of all them that were in the synagogue were fastened on him.

And he began to say unto them, This day is this Scripture fulfilled in your ears.

And all bare him witness, and wondered at the gracious words which proceeded out of his mouth. And they said, Is not this Joseph's son?

And he said unto them, Ye will surely say unto me this proverb, Physician heal thyself: whatsoever we have heard done in Capernaum, do also here in thy country.

And he said, Verily I say unto you, No prophet is accepted in his own country.

But I tell you of a truth, many widows were in Israel in the days of Elias, when the heaven was shut up three years and six months, when great famine was throughout all the land;

But unto none of them was Elias sent, save unto Sarepta, a city of Sidon, unto a woman that was a widow.

And many lepers were in Israel in the time of Eliseus the prophet; and none of them was cleansed, saving Naaman the Syrian.

And all they in the synagogue, when they heard these things, were filled with wrath,

And rose up, and thrust him out of the city, and led him unto the brow of the hill whereon their city was built, that they might cast him down headlong.

But he, passing through the midst of them, went his way."
(Luke 4:16-30)

What is the situation once again with the perfect Human Being himself?

A covenant man with no Sin attached to his being, is directed by the unction of the Holy Spirit of God, to declare Scriptural truth, and in so doing is taking his first official step into public ministry. Here, the armour pieces used would be:

Jesus is a man whose **(1)** loins are *girt about with truth*. He is a **(2)** *righteous* man preaching that the kingdom of heaven is at hand. He is a man of **(3)** *faith* and has been able to defeat the works of darkness thus far at every turn. The **(4)** *sword of the spirit* emanates out of his mouth as he only speaks what God tells him to speak. He is an example of a man wearing the full *"Armour of God"* that has been made available to men.

What *"Weapons of Hell"* were being employed by the kingdom of darkness against him on this occasion?

(1) Circumstances - It is time for Jesus to publicly announce himself as the Messiah. The synagogue in the town where he was raised-up is the determined place. At first, the people graciously listened to what he had to say. As he spoke the truth concerning the stiff-necked and gainsaying of the Jewish people the tone of the crowd changed. Did Jesus purpose to provoke them? No, not necessarily, he is simply stating the factual truth. Did the possibility of them becoming provoked stop Jesus from telling them the truth? No, it did not. What began as a neutral or even positive circumstance, morphed rapidly into negative circumstances concerning this *announcement* issue.

(2) Fears - As the people become hostile they congeal into a *lynch mob* mind-set, determined to put a stop to this radical upstart. Personal convictions of the members of the synagogue, being confronted with truth, will trigger fear within them of being wrong, and ignite other emotions to erupt into actions. Did their zealous negative tone set a stage for Jesus himself to be tempted with fear of what they might do? Yes, it did. Is it possible that being surrounded by a hostile crowd of people pushing Jesus toward a well-known ledge, might cause his mind to race with thoughts of whatever possible options he may have for deliverance . . . because he has no disciples with him at this time to speak up for him or to defend him? Yes, it is possible.

(3) Emotions - The emotions of the people within the synagogue were quite tranquil when he read the Scripture, and began to expound. As he touched upon spiritual truth and factual events, the conviction that light brings when darkness is exposed, caused a flood of emotions to erupt to a disastrous level. Driven by these emotions, usually calm individuals begin to think, speak, and act contrary to that which they know to be right and true.

(4) People - Covenant people of God, who under normal conditions, would be more emotionally constrained because of the influence of the Law of Moses in their lives, become emotionally inflamed and choose to behave as perfect stooges for the devil because of their religious zealousness. The increasing crescendo of emotions causes the grabbing and pushing of a man who has actually done them no harm. They are being stirred to anger because what they choose to 'believe' deep down within their hearts is being challenged. Is it possible for *nice* people to suddenly become *not nice* when things do not go the way they want them to go, or that they thought might progress a different way? Yes, it is possible.

(5) Words - As in any given incident of warfare words are going to be spoken. Sometimes those words will be recorded within the Scriptures, sometimes they will not be recorded. But you can be sure that with heated emotions, words were spoken by those residents of Nazareth. And those words were possibly not particularly complimentary. Might those words be used to gender fear? Yes, they might. Might those words be filled with unrighteous emotions? Yes, they might. In any event, this situation looks fairly grim for Jesus.

What *"Weapons of Our Warfare"* are active in this example of assault against Jesus?

(1) The Word of God - Jesus quoted the word of truth. And even though the men of the synagogue did not like what followed the reading of Isaiah, the word of truth was declared and entered into their ears.

(2) Faith - Jesus was a man of faith. Jesus trusted his Father in heaven, he did not just hope that this will work out. He is familiar with *"Because thou hast made the Lord,* which is *my refuge,* even *the Most High, thy habitation; There shall no evil befall thee, neither shall any plague come nigh thy dwelling."* (Psalm 91:9-10)

(3) The Baptism of the Holy Spirit *(I Corinthians 12:7-11)(Acts 4:13)* Boldness - Jesus is the perfect example that we have, concerning a Human Being walking in the full effectiveness of the cloaking of the Holy Spirit.

Jesus lived and ministered exclusively under the direction of the Holy Spirit of God. He fully submitted himself to whatever guidance the Holy Spirit would give unto him as to what he was to say and what he was to do.

He was an open vessel through which the Holy Spirit was able to execute His diversities of gifts, differences of administrations, and diversities of operations.

The *Discerning of spirits, Word of Wisdom* and *Faith* gifts are in operation within this incident.

In the natural, Jesus is being gruffly shuffled out of the synagogue and toward the **"brow of the hill"** *(Luke 4:29)* drop-off by many participating hands. Suddenly, having received instruction from the Holy Spirit he abruptly stops and stands erect, which potentially startles his accusers. He turns to face the angry crowd, and with confidence from the gifted faith looks them squarely in the eyes, and then sets his own eyes on the far side of the tumult. Without saying a word, he confidently strides through the cluster of emotion and outrage and emerges on the other side. Despite the jeers and the catcalls that follow, he briskly continues to walk to the outskirts of the town and disappears into the surrounding countryside.

Jesus did his part, God did his part, and the result was again, deliverance and victory. If God be for us, who can be against us?

(5) PETER DELIVERED FROM PRISON

"Now about that time Herod the king stretched forth his hand to vex *certain of the church.*

And he killed James the brother of John with the sword.

And because he saw it pleased the Jews, he proceeded further to take Peter also. (Then were the days of unleavened bread.)

And when he had apprehended him, he put him *in prison, and delivered* him *to four quaternions of soldiers to keep him* (four teams of four soldiers in each team. Chained to two and guarded by two)*; intending after Easter to bring him forth to the people.*

Peter therefore was kept in prison: but prayer was made without ceasing of the church unto God for him.

And when Herod would have brought him forth, the same night Peter was sleeping between two soldiers, bound with two chains: and the keepers before the door kept the prison.

And, behold, the angel of the Lord came upon him*, and a light shined in the prison: and he smote Peter on the side, and raised him up, saying, Arise up quickly. And his chains fell off from* his *hands.*

And the angel said unto him, Gird thyself, and bind on thy sandals. And so he did. And he saith unto him, Cast thy garment about thee, and follow me.

And he went out, and followed him; and wist not that it was true which was done by the angel; but thought he saw a vision.

When they were past the first and the second ward, they came unto the iron gate that leadeth unto the city; which opened to them of his own accord: and they went out, and passed on through one street; and forthwith the angel departed from him.

And when Peter was come to himself, he said, Now I know of a surety, that the Lord hath sent his angel, and hath delivered me out of the hand of Herod, and from all the expectation of the people of the Jews.

And when he had considered the thing, he came to the house of Mary the mother of John, whose surname was Mark; where many were gathered together praying.

And as Peter knocked at the door of the gate, a damsel came to hearken, named Rhoda.

And when she knew Peter's voice, she opened not the gate for gladness, but ran in, ad told how Peter stood before the gate.

And they said unto her, Thou art mad. But she constantly affirmed that it was even so. Then said they, It is his angel.

But Peter continued knocking: and when they had opened the door, and saw him, they were astonished.

But he, beckoning unto them with the hand to hold their peace, declared unto them how the Lord had brought him out of the prison. And he said, Go show these things unto James, and to the brethren. And he departed, and went into another place.
(Acts 12:1-17)

So, what is the warfare situation here within the Book of Acts?

The existing established government begins to take adverse action against the increasingly unpopular constituency of Christian believers in Jerusalem. James, the son of Zebedee, who was a follower of Jesus of Nazareth was targeted and subsequently killed with a sword. A second New Creation leader is arrested as a 'show of force' from the existing governing establishment, with the intentions of bringing him before a group of people who would gladly consent unto his death.

Which implements of the *"Armour of God"* will Peter be protected by, whether consciously or unconsciously?

(1) Belt of Truth - Peter is speaking the truth at every opportunity. He has been preaching the truth, concerning what God did through Jesus Christ of Nazareth on the cross of Calvary, everywhere that the Holy Spirit of God has taken him.

(2) Breastplate of Righteousness - Peter is actively walking in whatever amount of light that he has from God's word. He is choosing to obey God's instructions in all things. By being 'in Christ', he has legally become the righteousness of God.

(3) Preparation of the Gospel of Peace - Peter is ever learning who he is *in Christ* and is always ready to give an answer to every person that asks him the reason for the hope that they see in him.

(4) Shield of Faith - Peter has placed his faith in what God has said is so, regardless of what is happening all around him.

(5) Helmet of Salvation - After walking closely with Jesus for an extended period of time, Peter is fully persuaded concerning Christ and is in an on-the-job process of fully learning who he is *in Christ*.

What *"Weapons of Hell"* are once again being mobilized against an individual resident of the kingdom of light? Invalid memories?—No. Physical handicaps?—No.

(1) Circumstances - The religious and political climate has shifted in Jerusalem. Upon the death of Stephen, the disciples were scattered, but the apostles remained in the city. At a point in time, Satan moved upon the king, and the scales were tipped, and another believer in Jesus was murdered. The response from the 'people' was a positive response, so Herod was embolden to strike again, and Peter was arrested. He also was due to be murdered shortly.

(2) Fears - The gospel is contrary to Judaism in many ways. Jesus of Nazareth was considered to be a radical, and those that followed him were perceived no differently. The fervor of what his death accomplished continues to grow even unto today. Fear of traditions being set aside, and the long established Law of Moses being challenged during the days that we are observing, is increasing. The indiscriminate death of James without hesitation sets a tone in the city. Being arrested with the knowledge that he is to be brought before Herod and ultimately killed, presents Peter with the opportunity to be quite fearful. The believers also are tempted to fear concerning what the future would hold, should another leadership icon suffer death at the hands of the king.

(3) Emotions - Satan is able to successfully use hatred, anger, jealousy, wrath, variance, and strife, just to name some emotions within this Biblical incident. Herod is stirred. The people are stirred. Other prisoners are stirred. And Peter is certainly going to be tempted to become emotionally stirred. Tensions are running high.

(4) People - Israel is the land of people who believe in, and are in a Blood Covenant relationship with, the One True God. The religious rulers and representatives of God on earth were individuals who had declared with their positions and actions that, *"we see"*. *(John 9:41)* Even though Herod was politically aligned with Rome, he was still of an Israelite heritage and was a Jewish man. What seems to be wrong with this picture? What is manifest is, Light vs. Darkness. People of darkness, even though they may not know that they are people of darkness, are at war with the people of light. And *Hell* will use any soldier it can enlist to achieve its goal.

(5) Words - Undoubtedly, words were spoken during the assault and death of James. The people certainly expressed their support and endorsement of what Herod did with words. Declarations of what Herod intended to do with Peter were conveyed with words as well. Fear would take the opportunity to tempt Peter with the words that were being spoken during all of this turmoil. And if there were any other prisoners that Peter came into contact with, their words too would add to the spiritual weight of the situation.

What *"Weapons of our Warfare"* are we able to identify during this assault?

(1) Faith - Although we have no words spoken by Peter to confirm this, Peter has been privy to many things in connection with Jesus. There would be a definite temptation to be quite anxious, but Peter is going to believe that God will somehow deliver him. Since there is nothing that he can do personally, he will simply rest in the confidence that he has in God.

(2) Prayer - Members of the Body of Christ are aware of what has happened to Peter. Word of what has happened goes out, and there is a gathering together of believers to petition God for Peter's release. Either two standing in agreement, or one effectually, fervently praying should do the trick.

(3) Holy Angels - While Peter lay trustingly in a state of sleep, an angel of the Lord was dispatched in response to the prayers, and his intervention caused supernatural chain and lock releases. Peter himself was not even fully aware of what was happening until it was all but over.

(4) Words - Words of instruction and deliverance were uttered unto Peter from the angel. Words of petition were uttered by the believer's unto a loving God of mercy. Words of testimony were uttered by Peter to the gathered believers upon his release.

A very real incident with potentially devastating consequences was turned completely around, demonstrating the triumphing of good over evil. As it was occurring, in real time, were the individuals involved checking off, in their minds, the ordered steps that they needed to follow from their spiritual warfare training classes in order to be victorious? Probably not. Were they aware that spiritual issues is where the rubber-meets-the-road and that they really do affect the end result of either life or death? Definitely yes. Had prayer not been offered, and faith in the surety of God's deliverance not been believed and released, would the outcome of the incident have been different or the end results remain the same? Very possibly different.

Light verses darkness; good verses evil; blessings verses curses; right verses wrong; truth verses lies; and on and on are the things that we are dealing with from day to day. The devil and the powers of hell take it quite seriously, and we should as well.

(6) PAUL, THE SHIP, AND THE STORM

"And when the south wind blew softly, supposing that they had obtained their purpose, loosing thence, they sailed close by Crete.

But not long after there arose against it a tempestuous wind, called Euroclydon.

And when the ship was caught, and could not bear up into the wind, we let her drive.

And running under a certain island which is called Clauda, we had much work to come by the boat:

Which when they had taken up, they used helps, undergirding the ship; and, fearing lest they should fall into the quicksands, struck sail, and so were driven.

And we being exceedingly tossed with a tempest, the next day they lightened the ship;

And the third day we cast out with our own hands the tackling of the ship.

And when neither sun nor stars in many days appeared, and no small tempest lay on us, all hope that we should be saved was then taken away.

But after long abstinence, Paul stood forth in the midst of them, and said, Sirs, ye should have hearkened unto me, and not have loosed from Crete, and to have gained this harm and loss.

And now I exhort you to be of good cheer: for there shall be no loss of any man's life among you, but of the ship.

For there stood by me this night the angel of God, whose I am, and whom I serve,

Saying, Fear not, Paul; thou must be brought before Caesar: and, lo, God hath given thee all them that sail with thee.

Wherefore, sirs, be of good cheer: for I believe God, that it shall be even as it was told me.

Howbeit we must be cast upon a certain island.

But when the fourteenth night was come, as we were driven up and down in Adria, about midnight the shipmen deemed that they drew near to some country;

And sounded, and found it twenty fathoms: and when they had gone a little further, they sounded again, and found it fifteen fathoms.

Then fearing lest we should have fallen upon rocks, they cast four anchors out of the stern, and wished for the day.

And as the shipmen were about to flee out of the ship, when they had let down the boat into the sea, under colour as though they would have cast anchors out of the foreship,

Paul said to the centurion and to the soldiers, Except these abide in the ship, ye cannot be saved.

Then the soldiers cut off the ropes of the boat, and let her fall off.

And while the day was coming on, Paul besought them all to take meat, saying, This day is the fourteenth day that ye have tarried and continued fasting, having taken nothing.

Wherefore I pray you to take some meat; for this is for your health: for there shall not a hair fall from the head of any of you.

And when he had thus spoken, he took bread, and gave thanks to God in presence of them all; and when he had broken it, he began to eat.

Then were they all of good cheer, and they also took some meat.

And we were in all in the ship two hundred threescore and sixteen souls.

And when they had eaten enough, they lightened the ship, and cast out the wheat into the sea." (Acts 27:13-38)

In this last example that we are looking at from the Scriptures, what is the situation?

A covenant man under arrest from an unrighteous governmental agency is being transported internationally from his home country to the headquarters of a foreign government. During this transportation process, he is caught in the middle of a "natural disaster."

What portions of the *"Armour of God"* is this covenant man protected with?

(1) Loins Girt About With Truth - Paul has learned through instruction what the real 'truth' is concerning established spiritual issues. He is purposing to utilize every opportunity to speak that truth to every individual that he comes into contact with. The protection that he receives is the direct covering of the Holy Spirit of Truth Himself.

(2) The Breastplate of Righteousness - Paul is actively walking in the light of God's word, and actively receiving and choosing to obey His instructions in all things. He is secure in his legal righteousness by being *in Christ*, and in his behavioral aspect by his obedience to the Holy Spirit's directives.

(3) His feet are Shod With the Preparation of the Gospel of Peace - Paul knows who he is in Christ Jesus, and is always ready to give an answer to every man that asks him the reason for the hope that they see in him.

(4) He is Taking the Shield of Faith, *"Wherewith He is Able to Quench All the Fiery Darts of the Wicked".* *(Ephesians 6:16)* Paul has chosen to place his trust in, and believe, what God has stated is so . . . in spite of what other evidence may present itself. For Paul, the word of God takes precedence over all of the circumstances, fears, other people, or words that he may hear.

(5) The Helmet of Salvation - Paul is knowledgeable of, and fully persuaded, concerning his position in Christ. And he has cried out unto the Lord, *"that I may know him, and the power of his resurrection".* *(Philippians 3:10"* Christ Jesus is all things to Paul, and he will not allow anything that this earth may have to distract him.

Paul is fully clothed in an armour that he never takes off. And the protection that that armour affords him preserves him even in dire circumstances.

What *"Weapons of Hell"* does the devil draw on in this incident of attempted 'steal, kill, and destroy' conflict? Invalid memories? - No. Physical handicaps? - No.

(1) Circumstances - On a ship at sea, Paul is a captive prisoner. A stirring of the natural and the mustering up of a hurricane carries more than enough power to destroy the ship and every passenger on it. For two weeks, the pilgrims are locked into the wind and rain fury of *Euroclydon.*

(2) Fears - The ship that they were on was not a well-sized cruise ship. It was a modest size vessel, but the passenger complement was an unusually heavy 276 persons, not even considering the additional weight of the cargo and the tackling. Thoughts of floundering pummeled the Apostle on a regular basis. The reactions of the sailors and soldiers to the circumstances were potentially of no benefit either. There was ample opportunity for fear to be gendered from any number of sources.

(3) Emotions - Going through a tropical hurricane, within very confined quarters, amidst a couple of hundred people, with no place to escape to, is bound to stir up some emotions. Fear, impatience, anger, frustration, and a feeling of hopelessness and abandonment can mount up quite quickly. Pitting men one against another within an emotional crucible of pressure, within Satan's eyes, is going to produce a bumper crop of death.

(4) People - Of the 276 persons on board the ship less than a handful would not be enlisted as active agents of doom and gloom. Most certainly the circumstances and attending pressures and fears would motivate their behavior.

(5) Words - Words carry power. Words convey fears. Words express anger. Words generate a composite for inappropriate thoughts, and then those thoughts are expressed and invested power released through more words. One can only imagine the incredible amount of negativity and destruction that may have been released through words over a two week inundation of potential death hanging like a cloud over head.

And so, what **"Weapons of Our Warfare"** might we see actively being employed within this final example? The word of God? - There is no record of Scripture being spoken, but Paul is a man knowledgeable of the word of God, and there is ample opportunity for him to bring it to bear on the situation. The name of Jesus? - Again, there is no record. But Paul is the one who tells us that in all that we say or do . . . it should be done in the name of the Lord Jesus. The blood of the Lamb? —No record of the application of the blood.

(1) Faith - Paul is walking in demonstrated trust. The Shield of Faith is protecting him and working on his behalf, and we do have recorded **"for I believe God"** *(Acts 27:25)* within the midst of all of the turmoil that was going on around him. Paul's faith was being released, and he was receiving what he was believing for.

(2) Prayer - Although there is not a record of out-right prayer being made, we do have the notation of the angelic visitation and the breaking of bread within the incident records. We are able to draw from those two events, the very real probability that Paul petitioned God, through prayer, for the safety of all of the other passengers on board the vessel. And most probably prayed that he might receive clarity of instruction from the Lord on what to do, step by step.

(3) Angels - Once again we have angelic intervention in a New Testament event. And we are not seeing this just because Peter and Paul are the Apostles of the Lord. The Scriptures declared that angels are all ministering spirits sent forth to minister for them who shall be the heirs of salvation. *(Hebrews 1:14)* So we are able to be in expectation of angelic intervention on our behalf as well, should the situation call for it.

(4) Words - Amidst the plethora of negative words that may have been swirling around, Paul received encouraging words from the angel that visited him. He then turned around and spoke those same positive words to the men in the ship. And in verse 36 when we find that they were all of good cheer, some words of value and importance may have been spoken.

In the natural, a situation like this incident carries with it an *it's all over* tone to it. But we serve a God of mercy and deliverance. So the seeming impossibility of the circumstances is not the bottom line.

We see that Paul maintained a consistency throughout this entire episode. He relays to the men in charge that they should have listened to him in the first place, and saved themselves the distress and financial loss. However, he does not gloat "I told you so" or "you are getting what you deserve" to them. Rather he has been believing on God for deliverance, and because of that, he was saved, and no one else lost their life either.

We have taken the opportunity to observe six incidents within the pages of Scripture in which we can clearly see the validity of the **"Armour of God"** that we have been given, the real **"Weapons of Hell"** that a formidable enemy has and uses, and finally the **"Weapons of Our Warfare"** that are mighty through our God unto victory.

We shall conclude our study by noting some everyday issues that we deal with in this 21st century.

21st Century Everyday Warfare

The last segment of this study that we want to look at is the everyday issues that members of the Body of Christ currently face in this rubber-meets-the-road day and age in which we live.

We will examine ten various subjects. And we will touch upon numerous points under each of those main subject headings that may apply in more detail to those subjects.

At the outset, so that we do not have to refer back to our basics after each category evaluation, we need to determine as to whether or not **#1 -** Our *"Armour of God"* is in place . . . **#2 -** ascertain what *"Weapons of Hell"* might be in operation . . . and **#3 -** be mindful of and be willing to put to use the *"Weapons of Our Warfare"*. Remember, *"If God be for us, who can be against us?"* (Romans 8:31) and prevail?

(1) SICKNESS AND/OR DISEASE

1. An ill individual is being subjected to an outright assault of sickness or disease from hell.

The number one *observable* end-result of the finished work of Christ Jesus on the cross is physical health. The Bible declares clearly that physical bodily health is a finished work product of redemption. *(Isaish 53:4-5; Psalms 107:20; Proverbs 4:22; I Peter 2:24; James 5:14-15)* And it is Satan that will use sickness and disease not only to steal from the individual that is being afflicted, but to attempt to put forth a visible notice to the whole world that shouts "this Bible stuff" does not actually work! In addition, Satan has managed successfully to enlist into his campaign Born-Again New Creations. He has convinced a good percentage of professed Christianity that "God does not necessarily heal everybody" but rather only a select few.

There is no Scriptural indication anywhere that there is going to be another work done at another time, that is going to deal with and finally take care of the ill-health problem. The work is already done. Whatever sickness or disease may be attempting to assault you is not something that finds its origin with God. If you are a Born-Again New Creation, then **you were healed** two thousand years ago by the stripes that Jesus of Nazareth took upon his body during his passion and crucifixion.

However, today if a person chooses to **believe** that they are sick, or that they have a particular disease, then the operational laws of the Universe, and the declaration of Jesus' statement that people get to have whatever it is that they choose to believe for, does indeed become quite real in their life. *(Mark 11:24)*

Now, please do not allow any place for condemnation in your life at the hearing of that statement. *(Romans 8:1)* For some people, to receive the revelation that Jesus paid the full price for sickness and disease, and to receive the free gift from God of His divine healing, is not a difficult issue. For other people, it is not an easy situation to deal with at all. Because, pain is real. Diagnosis from the doctor is real. Physical evidence that something is amiss is real. And many times these *signs* are overwhelming and persuasive.

A quality decision is going to become necessary. Should a person desire to walk in divine healing and divine health, it is obtainable. However, a pro-active position is what is called for. And if there is no deviation from that position, then success will be the end result.

2. Displayed open rebellion and disobedience to the word of God leads to a door being opened for an attack from hell.

Our God prefers obedience instead of sacrifice. He has given us His word as the bottom-line instructions for all things that pertain to life and godliness. *(II Peter 1:3)* God tells us that his commandments are not grievous. *(I John 5:3)* So, there is unquestionably no justifiable reason for our knowing, willing disobedience. We are the ones that choose to rebel.

When we become aware of this, and we opt to remain willingly ignorant of spiritual truths, then it is not God's fault should something attack us physically. Disobedience of any kind leaves an open door for assault and an invitation for hell to impose upon us whatever it has been cooking up for us on the front burner.

3. The actual spirit of infirmity has somehow gained entrance to your being and is launching an assault against your body.

The spirit of infirmity is one of fifteen named spirits that operate within the kingdom of darkness. The speciality of the spirit of infirmity is diseases or illnesses that linger over extended time. Cancer, Emphysema, Asthma, Lupus, etc., and the full contingent of allergies of every kind.

Having a lingering disease does not necessarily mandate that the spirit of infirmity is the root cause of the problem because universal laws are also involved. However, when the root cause of the problem **is** ultimately the spirit of infirmity, then Christ-provided authority can terminate the maneuvers and activities of the spirit of infirmity or attending spirits of darkness, and healing will be the end result.

4. A displayed free-will ignorance of natural laws that are known to lead to illness when disobeyed open doors.

When you were young, your mother told you to put on your coat and your galoshes if you were going to go out into the cold or into the rain. When you chose to ignore your mother's advice, and just do what you wanted to do, then quite often, sickness and misery was the end result.

Things have not actually changed very much. We still become knowledgeable of certain natural laws, and the consequences of breaking those laws, and yet we choose to do our own thing. When that occurs, potential sickness and/or disease may be the end result.

5. A person exercising a genuine belief in sickness and disease, and a willingness to receive whatever may come their way, usually gets it.

Many people exercise a real belief in sickness and disease. They do not like the consequences of what sickness and disease produces, but they still personally believe that there is not much that they can do about it. 'Everybody has to get sick at some time' would be the mantra that they might chant. And when a 'common cold' comes drifting down the lane, instead of allowing it to go right by, they choose to catch it.

The work of the cross and the spiritual reality that that work has provided for, are not even part of their thinking, even though they are a Christian. They are so used to sickness and disease simply being a viable part of life that they unconsciously exercise a real belief in its validity. *(Mark 11:24)*

And the sad truth is that sickness and disease are very real. But they belong to the plethora of rules, regulations, and consequences that govern and affect the kingdom of darkness. These individuals are residents of that kingdom and captives to the Law of Sin. If you are a Born-Again New Creation, then you have been delivered from that kingdom, and translated into the kingdom of God's dear Son. *(Colossians 1:13)* And you now have a new set of rules, regulations, and consequences that you are to follow and benefit from, and sickness and disease are not a part of them.

So, how do we win?

It starts with a deep, genuine, desire to be victorious. If you are going to exercise a half-hearted effort for whatever reason, it will not do the trick. We must be quite serious about defeating darkness, and genuinely willing to become pro-active, or we will not succeed.

The foundation for victory of every single incident of combat is going to be the word of God. **God has declared what is so, and that is it.** Declared truth **is** a spiritual reality, and it does not change.

It is God's perfect will for you to be healed, if you are sick. Sometimes your healing will come forth instantly, and sometimes there will be a 'time' factor involved. During that 'time' factor, there will be a temptation to give in to what your body is saying to you. **Do Not Do That.**

God is the **highest authority** on the subject of health and healing: not your doctor, not your friends, not your relatives, and not even your own body. You must purpose to refuse to believe what you may see or feel. You must purpose to refuse to doubt as to whether or not the word of God is actually working. You must refuse to waver from what God declares.

Go to the Scriptures. Find the God declared truth concerning divine healing and health. Write these Scriptures down so that you will have them with you always.

If medication is involved, continue to take the medication until the Spirit of Truth bears witness with your spirit that you can discontinue the medication. However, during this process do not choose to exercise your belief in whatever sickness or disease may be involved.

Confession **always** comes before possession, so you need to declare with your own mouth what the word of God states, before you actually have the manifestation of it. It is very detrimental for you to simply confess how you feel. Truth is not affected by 'feelings', but the 'feelings' ultimately will be affected by the truth. Take your stand on truth, and do not allow yourself to be detoured, no matter how long it may take. Truth + Consistency + Faith = Divine Healing.

(2) NUANCES OF THOUGHTS, WORDS, AND DEEDS

1. The subtlety of unrighteous thoughts.

"For as he thinketh in his heart, so is *he:"* (Proverbs 23:7a)

The realm of thought is the primary realm of the three realms of existence. When God gave intelligence unto Man, the ability to think freely came with the intelligence package. When God gave a free-will unto Man, the capacity for personal desires came with the free-will package. The divine-design-intent was that unfettered thinking combined with insightful personal desires would produce creative vision. That vision would transition through the realm of word, into the realm of deed, and begin to bring forth new creation into God's Universe.

Before Man had ever come upon the scene, God had created angelic beings and gave them similar intelligence and free-will packages. However, they were not brought forth "in" the image or "after" the likeness of God, and could not ultimately create anything. We now have a Scriptural record that substantiates, that within the life of one particular angel, who had earned and carried the *creative anointing* of God Himself, (Ezekiel 28:14-15) thoughts were allowed to go renegade. And inappropriate personal desires combined with those thoughts, transitioned through the realm of word into the realm of deed, birthed forth iniquity, and the Law of Sin was the end product.

Upon the entrance of Man, Adam knowingly, consciously, and willingly disobeyed God. Following an established path of previous disobedience, he subsequently became a captive to that same Law of Sin.

Today, the word of God commands us to take control over our thoughts and bring them into subjection to God's directives. (II Corinthians 10:5) When we fail to do this, subtleties of unrighteousness begin to seep into our thinking and we have the very real opportunity of allowing renegade thoughts to adversely affect every area of our lives.

If we are *in Christ* then the spiritual reality is that we are dead to ourselves. Dead people do not have a capacity to think independently. Renegade thoughts should not be allowed to roam about freely and ultimately transition into words, and then potentially into deeds. They need to be pro-actively dealt with using the word of God, the name of Jesus, the blood of the Lamb, and other weapons that can pull these exalted thoughts down unto subjection to the new Born-Again Human spirit. And the Holy Spirit of grace will instruct each and every one of us, as to how we are uniquely, individually able to do that.

2. The subtlety of incorrect or idle words.

"Death and life are in the power of the tongue: and they that love it shall eat the fruit thereof." *(Proverbs 18:21)*

Words are going to be the result of a collage of thoughts. Words are going to frame desires and give a basis for actions. The word of God is a concise collection of words that are absolutely and perfectly harmonious in their totality. This is the reason that the Scriptures are referred to as the **word** of God, and not the **words** of God.

Whatever we have abundantly crammed into our heart up until this very point in time, is what will come out of our mouth in the form of words. No exceptions. What we truly are thinking deep down within our being, will gel into the words that we choose to speak, and will expose what is truly within the safe-deposit box of our heart.

We have been commanded to be mindful of what we say. *"Swift to hear, slow to speak,"* *(James 1:19)* We are to avoid allowing frivolous idle words to pour unrestricted out of our mouth. And at least one of the reasons for this is because words are creative. If we are not cautious, we could become guilty of moving our lips and bringing evil to pass. *(Proverbs 16:30)*

The Lord will help us to put a check on our mouth if we will but only ask him. Our language of necessity must be brought into subjection to our newly Born-Again spirit man, or we will be sowing verbal seeds that are unrighteous and vile into this already over corrupted world.

3. The subtlety of inappropriate actions.

"In this the children of God are manifest, and the children of the devil: whosoever doeth not righteousness is not of God,"
(I John 3:10)

Actions are destined to become the final resting place of thoughts, that most of the time have transitioned through words. The world that we live in actually declares that actions speak louder than words; however, that is only partially true. It is a toss-up as to what wreaks the most havoc: words or deeds. But the devastation that inappropriate actions can unleash is able to be visibly seen, and ripple outward much more readily than spoken words.

Words are designed to create, but they can effectively destroy as well. Actions are originally designed to be the result of creative words, but it was the knowing, willing, conscious, acting against that which was known to be right and true that birthed the blackest Law that ever 'saw-the-Light' into existence for evermore.

Men will act upon that which they believe. Change what a man thinks and you will change what that man believes. Change what that man believes and you will change not only what he says, but what he does as well.

To be sure, discipline is certainly involved. However, we have a new spirit, the full entourage of the gifts and power of the Holy Spirit, and the weaponry that our God has provided to help us get the job done. We can prevail. We must prevail, if we are going to keep the dogs-of-darkness at bay and bring glory and praise unto our God.

(3) FINANCIAL DISTRESS

The number two *observable* result of the finished work of Christ Jesus on the cross is for financial prosperity. The Scriptures present a clear case for blessing and prosperity for the people of God. *(Proverbs 10:22), (Psalm 112:3), (Ecclesiastes 5:19), (Philippians 4:19)* And since one of the primary maneuvers of the kingdom of darkness is to steal, Satan delights in keeping the children of God in an impoverished condition, so that the world will be able to see that "this Bible stuff" does not really work! He is able to accomplish this through ignorance of Biblical truth, unbelief, and willing disobedience.

1. Any person stealing from God by failing to tithe and return to God that which belongs to him, opens a way of attack.

"And all the tithe of the land whether of the seed of the land, or of the fruit of the tree, is the Lord's: it is holy unto the Lord." (Leviticus 27:30)

"Will a man rob God? Yet ye have robbed me. But ye say, Wherein have we robbed thee? In tithes and offerings." (Malachi 3:8)

The doctrine of the *tithe* precedes the Law of Moses by four hundred years plus.

The precedent for tithing is established within the Book of Genesis, during the dealings which took place between Abraham and Shem, the extremely elderly, and only surviving, middle son of Noah.

At the time of the event, there is no established Godly priesthood of any kind. Yet, carrying the title of Melchizedek, the righteous Shem is Scripturally declared to be *"the priest of the most high God."* (Genesis 14:18)

Jesus of Nazareth confirmed the validity of the tithe as he chastised the scribes and Pharisees. *(Matthew 23:23)* So the *tithe* is **not** an "Old Testament" doctrine that does not apply to the Born-Again, New Creation, Body of Christ.

God gave men the instructions concerning how to bring the tithe, within the Abrahamic Covenant, Mosaic Law guidelines it is true. *(Deuteronomy 26:1-3)* But that does not mean that God is obligated to re-invent the wheel in order to confirm and establish that the doctrine is valid, for New Testament individuals who are supposed to be *believers* and declare all the time that **"we see"**. *(John 9:41)*

When we do not return to someone, that which legitimately belongs to them, then we are stealing from them that which is not ours in the first place. The *tithe* or first-fruit of all that we have belongs unto the Lord. If we do not tithe, we are stealing from God, and classified as a thief . . . it is that simple.

2. Any person stealing from other people and putting a spiritual law *". . . for whatsoever a man soweth, that shall he also reap"* into operation. *(Galatians 6:7)*

The world calls it *karma* but it is actually a spiritual law. We are not supposed to covet or to take that which belongs to someone else. And when we do, we set a series of invisible wheels in motion which produce destructive results.

Financial provision and blessing from God are based upon unchangeable laws. God's desire is that we learn what these laws are, and then exercise them for our own benefit.

When we sow to unrighteousness, we put ourselves in a position to receive unrighteousness. Stealing from others is wrong, no matter how minor or *manini* it is. And it will cause existing laws to work against us.

3. Displayed disobedience or willing ignorance to the Biblical laws of sowing and reaping makes us vulnerable to attack.

8

Just as there are *sowing and reaping* laws concerning vegetation and natural growth, so there are also 'giving and receiving' laws when it comes to finances. *(Luke 6:38) (Philippians 4:15)*

Tithing is mandatory for covenant men and women and is not subject to discussion. But offerings are optional. Giving to the poor is the same as lending unto the Lord, and He will repay. *(Proverbs 19:17)*

Godly stewardship is the foremost consideration purpose for currency and financial exchange. And the word of God has ample instruction designed for our benefit. We would do well to pay heed to it and obey.

4. Any person can be a captive to *"the deceitfulness of riches"* that Jesus warned us about. *(Mark 4:19)*

The *"deceitfulness of riches"* does not simply apply to individuals that are well-to-do. A poor man can be consumed and affected with a lack of wealth, just as much as a rich man can be consumed and affected with too much wealth. A man might be willing to steal from, or to kill another man over even one dollar, just as readily as a man might be willing to steal from, or to kill another man over one million dollars. It is not the amount of money that is the problem, it is the attitude of the man.

When Born-Again New Creations put their trust in anything material for their provision, rather than in God, they become captives to the *"deceitfulness of riches"*. Jehovah Jireh is our source . . . not our savings account, or our job, or the government entitlement programs, or the stock market, nor any other potential material source.

Failure to know and to obey the financial laws is what will result in poverty and lack, not where the money is coming from.

5. Exercising a belief that there is demonstrated humility before God through financial lack and poverty.

The notion that financial lack demonstrates a humbleness before God is Biblically unsound and willfully ignorant in the process.

Within Judaism financial blessing was seen as a favorable condition with God. Jesus of Nazareth was a rich man contrary to what prevailing Biblical ignorance insists. *(II Corinthians 8:9)* That is why he had need for a treasurer to manage the money. *(John 12:6 & 13:29)* When Jesus was instructing the disciples through the questions that the rich young ruler posed he stated,

"And again I say unto you, It is easier for a camel to go through the eye of a needle, than for a rich man to enter into the kingdom of God." *(Matthew 19:24)*

The response from his disciples was one of surprise and amazement, **"Who then can be saved?"** *(Matthew 19:25)* God's blessing was seen as a natural result of being in a blood covenant relationship with the living God and of obedience to the conditions of that covenant.

Religious men that are Biblically ignorant have put their own spin on what they think pleases God. And then have attempted to impose those ideas onto the backs of millions of other men.

So, how do we win?

Again, we must become serious about defeating darkness, and willing to become pro-active in order to emerge victorious. This is a war. And as long as we are on this earth we are going to be in this war. Twenty-four hours a day, seven days a week, month in and month out, and year in and year out. The enemy is persistent.

However, we do not belong to his kingdom anymore. We have been delivered from one kingdom and translated into another. With tenacity and obedience we will overwhelmingly win.

Let us first check the condition of our Armour, make the necessary corrections and adjustments and move on to step two.

Repent of disobedience, ignorance, rebellion, and unbelief where necessary. Purpose to take God at His word and obey. Pay your tithe and become sensitive to the Holy Spirit of God's direction concerning free-will offerings and giving to the poor.

Go to the Scriptures. Locate the verses that apply to your financial condition. Learn the promises concerning tithing, sowing and reaping, giving and receiving, and other declarations of spiritual truth. Adopt these statements as belonging to you.

As you would do with physical healing, speak those things which be not as though they were. Pray and declare the answer, not the problem. It is of no benefit at all to agree with, and confirm, the existing poor condition circumstances.

Confession **always** comes before possession. Line up your conversation with Scriptural truth, and choose to believe God to do what He does best. Then act on these decisions. God will provide as He has promised.

(4) STRUGGLES WITH PORNOGRAPHY OR UNBRIDLED SEXUAL LUSTS.

1. A person's addiction to sexual compulsions of sight or touch wreaks havoc to themselves.

Addiction is addiction. Drugs, alcohol, tobacco, and gambling are not the only culprits within the arena of addiction. And, all addictions find their origins within the categories of the lust of flesh and the lust of the eyes.

Women are not exempt by any means, but the main constituency of offenders when it comes to pornography are boys and men.

It would seem that the female of the species is sexually aroused and stimulated by demonstrated tenderness, romance, suggestive playfulness, and foreplay through kissing and the gentle caressing afforded through touch.

It would also seem that the male of the species is sexually aroused and stimulated by suggested or actual female exposure, or by stark visual motion or still pictures, combined with the suggestion or opportunity to touch that which visually stimulates. That is the main reason that pornography is mostly geared toward the males.

God is the creator and author of sex. Sex is God's idea, not Man's. The primary purpose behind the invention of sex is for the pro-creation of the Human race throughout all of eternity. However, God has graciously made that necessity a pleasurable one for both parties.

More than once Satan has seized upon the opportunity which the instinctive compulsion that is in direct connection with sexual activity affords. He utilized that opportunity to attempt to thwart God's plan for a redeemer, in maneuvering fallen angels to cohabitate with Human women for the purpose of producing unredeemable offspring. *(Genesis 6:2 & 4)*

Within today's society, he continues to advertise, promote, and denigrate the female Human body for the purpose of exploitation and the eventual bondage to sin.

2. A person's compulsion to engage in sexual activity in an unnatural, or on an unusually frequent basis, indicates addiction.

"Marriage is honorable in all, and the bed undefiled: but whoremongers and adulterers God will judge." (Hebrews 13:4)

God has said that sexual activity, within the confines of a marriage covenant, is without restriction . . . as long as there is an agreement between the two partners on what occurs.

It is not of God for one partner to coerce or to compel the other partner to engage in un-agreed upon activities. That parameter applies whether we are talking about perversion activities or frequency. God has called us to peace and to harmony, and the spiritual depth involving the marriage covenant is designed by God to make what starts out as two individuals, to be more and more operative as one with each passing day. Respect for our covenant partner and open communication will go a long way in keeping the relationship pure and rich.

3. The ease of internet, cable, or digital sexual material access has expanded this sin.

Research statistics indicate that 40% of Christian ministers that were studied are involved with cable pornography when they are at conventions or seminars. If those statistics are indeed valid, then that is more than a shocking condition and utterly unacceptable. How many testimonies have bubbled to the surface, of various exposés within certain Christian ministries that involve a sexually moral failure.

Within this day and age it has become so much easier to obtain, or to become involved with, something that the Scripture clearly teaches is wrong, and yet there is such a driving compulsion behind it. Concerning spiritual warfare, this is a serious problem.

Willing exposure of our faults, *(James 5:16)* combined with godly counseling, and a determined self discipline will lead to ultimate victory.

(5) MARITAL DISCORD

1. The failure of the husband to love his wife and give himself for her, even as Christ loves the church leads to insecurity and pain.

Marriage is not a 50%—50% proposition. It is a 100%—100% commitment. Marriage is a seriously valid blood covenant agreement, made up between two separate, independent individuals, that blends them into a singular oneness in the sight of God and in line with spiritual truth.

The man carries the burden of responsibility for the union whether he likes it or he does not like it, or whether he wants to shoulder that weight of responsibility. God will definitely hold him accountable when the time comes. He is to provide for his wife and protect her in all of life's venues. He is the decreed provider and bread-winner. Within a Born-Again New Creation covenant relationship, he is also the priest and prophet of the household. He is to be Scripturally knowledgeable and sensitive to the personal guidance of the Holy Spirit. There is no Scriptural basis for the husband to attempt to take the Bible and lord it over his wife, demanding that she is to be submissive unto him. That is a doctrinal error of perception generated by carnally minded religious men, and it is an abomination before the Living God.

If he is indeed a Born-Again New Creation, then he is commanded by God to love his wife and give himself for her, even as Christ loves the church. *(Ephesians 5:25)*

2. The failure of the wife to submit herself unto her own husband as she would unto the Lord brings discord within the marriage.

Within the United States of America, the 21st Century presents to us the day of the independent woman. As assertive, bold, independent, and commanding, she does not need the help of anyone to survive. "I am woman"! has even been committed to song.

She has not been originally and divinely designed to behave that way, but many times she finds herself thrust into a position and into a situation that she does not desire and is not thoroughly prepared to handle. Ergo . . . in her own self defense she develops this boldness and assertiveness. The entire feminist movement of recent years is a demonstrated outcropping of this dilemma.

Her husband may be the one to abdicate his position of responsibility, and she is left to fill in the gap. She finds that she must make the decisions, remedy the difficulties, facilitate the repairs, and put on any number of other different hats.

However, all of this does not change the spiritual laws of the Universe. And, as a Born-Again New Creation, she must purpose to obey the heavenly instructions and not yield to the circumstances that swirl all around her.

3. There is a failure of the couple to submit themselves, one to the other, in the fear of God.

Many times the covenant union starts out harmoniously, and if the union is not nurtured and maintained, as any growing thing should be over a period of time it, can begin to drift into **my** half and **your** half. Instead of becoming more and more like one, there is a serious rift and separation begins to take place. As the emphasis on **my** half increases, I will usually dig my feet deeper into the bog of resistance, and the thought of submitting unto my covenant partner becomes distant, and ever-more foreign. From my perspective, I am the one who is correct, and it is my covenant partner that needs to take a real good look in the mirror, and change.

Pride, arrogance, rebellion, and disobedience to the word of God are many times in full blown manifestation. And since I do not really purpose to pray all that often, even for the people and the things that I personally like, I certainly am not going to pray (at least in any godly manner) for the various people and the things that I am increasingly disliking.

The answer to the whole problem, of course, is to divorce this obviously disobedient person, and look for someone new. Sound familiar?

4. When one or both persons, who claim to be Christians, continue to remain carnally minded and allow aspects of death to affect their covenant, it may crumble.

When we become a Born-Again Christian, we automatically become accountable in the eyes of God. We are commanded to renew our minds. We are commanded to put off the old man and put on the new. We are commanded to cleanse ourselves of all filthiness of the flesh and of the soul. We are commanded to lay aside every weight and the sin which doth so easily beset us. We are commanded to grow up into the things which govern life. And as we begin to adopt favorite Scripture verses and integrate them into our vocabulary and into our thinking processes we are declaring "we see", *(John 9:41)* just like the Pharisees did in Jesus' day.

For any marriage to endure over time and prosper, it requires effort. A Human/Satanic nature is self-centered, to say the least. Through the new birth, we have the privileged opportunity of becoming partakers of the divine nature of God. *(II Peter 1:4)* We are not supposed to remain carnally minded. With the help of the Holy Spirit of God, we are to change the way that we think. When we change the way that we think, it will automatically change what we choose to believe. When we change what we choose to believe, it will automatically change what comes out of our mouth. When we change what comes out of our mouth, it will automatically change what we ultimately receive.

". . . to be carnally minded is death;" *(Romans 8:6)* and we cannot afford to let death rule, or continue to affect the various issues of our lives. Renewing our mind is not an option or a suggestion, it is a command. And when we willingly refuse to do that, we disobey God, and there will be serious consequences.

5. Being in, or entering into, an *"unequally-yoked"* covenant relationship. *(I Corinthians 7:12-15)* **(By the way, these are not Scriptures that give a valid foundation for a divorce. Should the couple separate, God's best would dictate that the Christian remain single until the death of the covenant partner. Or else, they are to be reconciled.)**

Unequalled yoking can occur in business dealings, in close friendships, and in marriage covenants, just to name three. A marriage covenant is the most dangerous situation to find one's self unequally-yoked in. A marriage covenant goes beyond just the natural that is operating in the world around us. A marriage covenant is spiritual. Two people in agreement form a spiritual bond, and a **"so be it"** position of decree. Two people in agreement constitute an exponential ten-fold increase of authoritative power. Two people present a formidable offense against the kingdom of darkness.

If you find yourself in an unequally-yoked situation, do not simply resign yourself to it. And do not look for some way that you can *escape* from it. You made the decision in the first place, man-up to it.

Purpose to effectually pray, prophetically declare, believe on God, and positionally stand. Utilize the God-given weapons that you have. God will honor your position, and you may be pleasantly surprised as to your covenant partner's response.

6. There is an unwillingness of one or both persons to work through their difficulties and differences in order to honor God and the covenant that is in place.

This is possibly one of the biggest difficulties that we have within the Body of Christ today. The foremost thought within the mind of each Christian should be our desire to honor God. If there is an unequal yoke in place, the situation becomes more difficult. However, every genuine Christian that is involved in a marital covenant agreement should desire first and foremost, to honor God. More of Jesus and less of me, with each passing day, should be the foundational goal of every Christian.

The primary cause for the spiritual reality of this difficulty is always Self. "I am right and he, or she, is wrong" is positionally stated. "But pastor Rob, you don't understand what he did . . ." " Well Pastor Rob, if only she would . . ." and on and on it goes. Self, of course, is **never** in the position of error, it is always the other person's fault. "I am not the one that needs to change, they are."

As a consequence of this kind of position, strife and division, anger and frustration, and various other emotional upheavals prevail, and the prospect of real victory drifts further and further away with the passage of time.

Although it does not sound too practical because of what we have just discussed, and the known emotional resistance that there would be, nevertheless someone once said, "If you are going to fight anyway, then fight naked."

Victory is something that is possible. However, it is going to lay within the guidelines of humility, contriteness, and genuine love like that which flows forth from our God. Is our real desire to honor our God, or to get our own way? We will certainly make the choice . . . and we will receive the consequence of the choice that we make. That is how it works every single time.

(6) DIFFICULTIES IN INITIALLY FINDING, OR IN DEMONSTRATED DISSATISFACTION WITHIN, GAINFUL EMPLOYMENT

1. A person seemingly is unable to find gainful employment.

The economy of our country and the financial condition of the state in which we live are not supreme, even though it appears overwhelming. Neither is our God subject to the unfavorable conditions that we may find all around us.

We are in a covenant. When one covenant partner is experiencing difficulty, the other covenant partner comes to his rescue. God knows where all of the positions of gainful employment are. And God knows the gifts and talents that He has given unto each and every one of His children. And God knows how to orchestrate a connection between column A and column B. However, it is imperative that we do our part, and then believe that our God will provide as He has promised.

We need to examine the ads. We need to check on the availability of work. We need to pound-the-pavement and not wait for someone to come knocking on our door and to call us by name. We need to distribute our resume', and then follow that up with inquiry. And we need to present our petition before our God and exercise our faith.

Being in covenant with God decrees that we will find employment. However, refusing a legitimate position because "I am worth more money than that" or "that is not what I wanted to do" is bogus.

When we are unemployed, our eight-hour-a-day responsibility should be to locate employment. After we have already become gainfully employed, should we not care for the particular position that we hold for whatever reason, we may look for other work on our days off or in our spare time. Otherwise, we are to stay employed right where we are. If we get God involved and on the scene through prayer, He will provide.

2. There are difficulties with superiors or fellow laborers.

Most difficulties with fellow employees or with the one who is in charge, will find its real basis within the delusion of Self. There is still a case of too much of me, and not enough Jesus. There are indeed legitimate instances when the problem rightfully belongs to the other person. However, as a child of God we are called to live and behave according to a higher standard than the world. And the grace that God has afforded us should provide us with sufficiency to do our job 'as unto the Lord' and trust God to work out all of the anomalies of personality discrepancies.

3. There is a lack of interest in even working at any job.

"For even when we were with you, this we commanded you, that if any would not work, neither should he eat." (II Thessalonians 3:10)

An epidemic of lethargy is sweeping over this nation in these last days. The work ethic that once prevailed within this country has dissipated. Government entitlements seduce able bodied individuals to opt for 'free money' rather than to persevere unto righteousness and the fulfillment of that which they already know that they should do. That condition for a Christian is especially pathetic, and a crying shame.

We are currently in this world, but we are not supposed to be of this world. Remember . . . we are in a spiritual war. We can choose to follow the path of least resistance and 'when in Rome do as the Romans do', or rise up with the help of our God and forge ahead.

Discipline to motivate oneself is once again going to be in demand, but we also know that we *"can do all things through Christ which strengtheneth (us)"* (Philippians 4:13) if we will but only take advantage of it.

It is essential that we become contributing members of the society unto which we belong. Not only for our own financial sake, but for an example that others might be able to identify with and follow as well.

4. There is discrimination in any number of areas.

We have the privilege of living in a country that has definite laws concerning discrimination. And the number of those laws and the severity of the consequences of breaking those laws has increased within these last days. However, all of that is on a natural level.

As a Born-Again Christian we are called to live and to walk according to a different standard, and a higher level than the world around us. We are to respond to demonstrated injustice rather than to react to it. We ourselves are to demonstrate a Christ-like attitude and temperate behavior in the face of adversity. If a violation of the mentioned civil laws is evident and substantive, then we have a legal recourse available to us, and we should avail ourselves of established legalities. But our attitude and our conduct needs to remain consistent with the word of God. Our 'light' must so shine before men that they may see our good works and glorify our Father which is in heaven. The whole of our life in this world is now all about God and our representation of Him, and it is not about us anymore.

(7) DISOBEDIENT OR REBELLIOUS CHILDREN

1. The failure of the parents to bring up the child in the nurture and admonition of the Lord.

Youth has its share of pitfalls and inexperience is certainly one of them. Today, children are usually the ones who are producing other children.

And the children who are producing other children are themselves usually not brought up in the nurture and admonition of the Lord. So a standard household of godlessness is pretty much the norm.

God has designed the program so that infancy, adolescence, and advanced youth are a one-time adventure. How many adults when asked if they would like to be a teenager once again, and have a second shot at puberty, have soundly refused. So God got that one right.

As a result, the parent is the one that is supposed to be in charge. The system does not operate correctly if the inmates are running the asylum. And any parent who is knowledgeable of the One True God is admonished to raise their offspring within the shadow of covenant truth and teach them about God.

The quality that Abraham would teach his children, and his children's children, is what caught God's attention in the first place. God's desire is that we do the same.

2. There is active, known or unknown, operation of drugs or other addictive substances within the life of the child.

A targeted goal of Satan is to steal. Steal the heart and the hope of a parent for their child, and steal the life of the child in the process. Drugs are a dead-end street. Not just some drugs, but all drugs, every time. Alcohol, tobacco, and other addictive substances are dead-end streets as well. In fact, all addictions are dead-end streets.

The active operation of the ***"spirit of bondage"*** *(Romans 8:15)* will necessitate a pro-active spiritual warfare if victory is to be enjoyed. The addict is in a prison, and is unable to free themselves. They are a willing bond-slave to chemicals. They are a prisoner to an unquenchable driving force of ultimate death. Professional help from individuals who are indeed genuinely professional, and truly do know what they are doing, can be of some benefit. But unless the spiritual root source of the problem is definitively dealt with, it will only be a band-aid application at best.

3. There is not an exercising of God-ordained parental authority, and the inmates are being allowed to run the asylum.

It begins when they are very young. Their actions and antics seem quite cute at first, and even bring a smile and ultimately laughter to the scene. As the children age and the antics continue, sadly, the parent unconsciously learns to acquiesce and adjust to the subtlety of their unwitting rebellion. Tantrums and hissy-fits become effective tools to keep the parent in line. Hard-core discipline is out of the question because these are modern times, and this is the 21st century, not the Biblical dark ages. After all, they are just innocent children. Some appropriate 'time-out' should provide sufficient incentive for radical behavioral adjustment, shouldn't it? And as the clock continues to tick, there genuinely is a manifested adjustment . . . the parent is no longer in charge.

The now teenager is becoming delinquent, and the path of disobedience and rebellion gradually turns into crime and terror. A successful blight becomes imposed upon the whole of society, and the blame becomes attached to a lack of education, to poverty or poor environment, and social injustice, rather than spiritual mismanagement.

Should this behavior be allowed to continue unchecked, and be multiplied by thousands of Christian households, the generation that will eventually step up into the governance position shall bring us even one more step closer to Godlessness.

The word of God in prayer, released with genuine faith and the name of Jesus, can turn this picture around, if it is coupled with active parental responsibility. Is it a painless procedure? No. But determination and exercised importunity can drastically change the societal landscape.

4. There is an already developed disdain or contempt for the parent because of disrespect and rebellion.

There is such a thing as *tough love*. In order for *tough love* to work, the parent must put their foot down on continuing to allow disrespect and outright rebellion free reign. Programs have been developed to deal with specific difficult cases, but it is a spiritual war that we are in, and it only manifests itself in the natural to attempt to distract us from where we actually need to focus.

". . . The effectual fervent prayer of a righteous man availeth much." (James 5:16b) However, we **must** know our authority and whom it is that we are dealing with, and then exercise faith in God's ability to turn the situation around. He knows what every heart is crying out for and what they genuinely need. He also knows who would be the most likely person to get through to a closed-thinking mind-set. Patience, sensitivity to the leading of the Holy Spirit, and a willingness to act upon what God directs will produce results.

(8) A SPIRITUAL LACK-LUSTER OR APATHY IN ONE'S WALK WITH THE LORD

1. We are just not as interested in spiritual things as we once were.

Today we live in a cesspool of spiritual apathy within our society, and in general the society is moving further and further away from God. Just a few short years ago, although it had been waning, that which was known as the "Christmas Spirit" was still operating within our country. In many places that has now become a thing of the past and commercialism and political correctness has stepped into the driver's seat.

A blanket of spiritual slumber has settled upon the populous and interest in going to church, or Bible study, or special speaker events is gone. The latest CG saturated films or favorite can't-be-missed television programs have taken the place that God once held.

Biblical prophecy is being fulfilled right before our eyes almost every day. God is not willing that any should perish, so He has placed a clarion call to every believer, but many phones are being allowed to ring . . . and ring . . . and ring. Spiritual apathy and disinterest is become a disease and the infection is spreading rapidly.

If it is our genuine desire not to be consumed by this plague, then we are going to have to: #1 - make a quality decision to make changes, #2 - become pro-active in our spiritual warfare endeavors, #3 - get ourselves into a place where solid spiritual truths are being taught, and #4 - allow a trusted mentor to hold us accountable as we move from step to step on the staircase of measured spiritual growth.

A resurgence of spiritual interest is possible, however, it is going to require swimming against the tide to obtain it.

2. Our everyday life is almost prayerless.

Since prayer changes things and effectual fervent prayer avails much, the devil will do all that he can to keep us distracted with the business of day to day affairs so that we will make no contribution to the positive, concerning that which is happening all around us.

Every day we 'find time' to eat something. Every day we need to go to work or to take care of business. Every day we have places to go, and people to see, and things to do. And through it all we take little or no 'time' to pray because we are just too busy.

Each and every one of us manages to discipline ourselves to the affairs of this life that we have cultivated, even if we are an undisciplined person. So it is that we need to discipline ourselves to pray. Choose a time, choose a place, and discipline yourself to go there. Draft a list of items or people that are in need of prayer and spend time with God. It will not happen automatically. Water follows the path of least resistance, and so do undisciplined persons. Make yourself do what you know you must do. And begin to do it today.

3. Our faith has diminished, and we are believing more and more in what we see and hear.

"So then faith cometh by hearing, and hearing by the word of God." (Romans 10:17)

If we do not associate ourselves with the word of God on a regular basis our faith can and will be diminished.

A good healthy breakfast will fuel the machine of our body and send us on our way to accomplish the needed daily tasks set before us. However, before too much time has passed the nutrients from that breakfast have transitioned unto the outer-most of our bodily extremities and exhausted their value. A re-fueling of the machine is necessary if we hope to continue to meet our worldly obligations. Failure to do that will give way to the on-set of weakness, and continued failure to fuel the machine will ultimately lead to a diminishment of strength and ultimately death.

Spiritual issues are no different. The word of God is quick and powerful . . . it is alive. Ingesting the word of God will fuel the new Born-Again spirit man to accomplish the needed daily tasks set before us. However, like the natural, the living spiritual elements can also become exhausted and more fuel is needed or weakness will set-in. And if the spirit man is starved long enough, severe spiritual damage and even death can occur.

Establishing a consistent habit of reading and studying of the word of God will cause faith to be increased and aid us in taking our stand against the world of sight and sound.

4. We are becoming overwhelmed with the day to day circumstances swirling about us.

Circumstances are a major weapon within the arsenal of *Hell.* The **"god of this world"** *(II Corinthiansw 4:4)* will cause a tornado of *happenings* or *coincidences* to regularly occur if we seem to be subject to their influence. If we tend to react rather than to respond, then Satan will provide plenty of circumstances for us to react to.

As Christians, we are to live and walk by faith. If I am several years into being *in Christ* and I am still as motivated by what I see and hear as when I first got saved, when do I plan to begin to live and walk by faith? Will I begin this year? Next year? The year after that? When all of the difficulties and anomalies of life disappear? When?

We do have the power to change the *circumstances* around us. That occurs by believing in the heart and confessing with the mouth things that be not, as though they were. *(Romans 4:17)* However, that believing in the heart will not occur without a renewing of the mind onto what the unchanging word of God declares. We need to find purpose, and to take action that will bring about change. Endeavor to make a decision, and then step by step follow through on that decision using the godly instructions that are made available to us.

(9) LACK OF CONFIDENCE IN GOVERNMENTAL OPERATION

1. We find ourselves living within a country that we believe is headed in the wrong direction.

It should not come as a surprise for us to hear that we are in the last days. The Bible has given us a description of these days in which we live, even from centuries ago, and as we see the fulfillment of prophecy right before our eyes, our attention should be turned unto things above for clear direction concerning the remaining days that lay ahead.

The major constituency of the populace of this country has, in the last few years, elected and put into positions of authority, men and women of unrighteousness. Far too many Christians participated in this error because of a focus on things on the earth rather than a focus on the things above. As a result, we have men and women actively leading us down the primrose path of economic destruction with a smile on their face. And for some people, it might necessitate the driving off of a cliff before they finally wake-up and recognize their error. Sadly, by then it will be far too late.

As men and women who say that **"we see"**, *(John 9:41)* the responsibility of sound, stable government, rests within our hands. This is something that goes far beyond political party preference. We must prayerfully consider the moral fiber and character behavior of those who are vying to represent us because their root beliefs will seep out into, and influence, the society to which we belong. Should we choose to bury our head in the sand, or tenaciously hold to an unrighteous position, then destruction will be the destined outcome.

Pro-active spiritual warfare with obedience to Biblical instruction will see a positive change come about in those who carry authority over us.

2. There are men and women of unrighteousness exercising blanket authority.

We are the ones who have placed these individuals in their positions of influence, and we have the responsibility of removing them when their openly anti-Biblical behavior bubbles to the surface. The world does not know the intricacies of the realm of the spirit, but Christians proclaim that they do.

Once again, pro-active spiritual warfare with obedience to Biblical instruction will see a positive change in those who hold this authority over us.

3. There are local civil servants moving contrary to the law abiding, and failing to move against the unrighteous and lawless.

The legal fabric within the United States of America is deteriorating at an alarming rate. Male and female judges, put into positions to render righteous judgments, have become increasingly disappointing in their unrighteous renderings. The average citizen is moving into a hopeless condition because there is no one to officially stand-up for them, and into the gap, to help them. As a country, we are on a path to revolution and anarchy if there are not serious changes made before too much more time goes by.

Local law enforcement individuals, at least within the arena of what we are locally familiar with, are lackadaisical in their duties. It is so much easier, and so much more lucrative, to inflict penalties for truly ludicrous violations on the average citizen, rather than tracking down the transgressing criminal for his blatant violation of the average citizen.

Prayer is the genuine answer to the problem; however, the bulk of the people who say that they pray are usually praying in unbelief. This statement is not made to be disrespectful in any manner. Why we think that good intentions or emotional content, instead of faith, is what

God bases His responses on, is certainly beyond this author's understanding.

May we purpose to gird up our loins and take on the challenge that is set before us. "Without any changes there will be no change" becomes more and more profound. May we purpose to make changes in line with Biblical direction.

(10) DEALING WITH FLAKY CHRISTIANS — BOTH WITHIN THE GENERAL BODY-OF-CHRIST AND WITHIN THE LEADERSHIP

1. Responding to self proclaimed Apostles, Prophets, Evangelists, Pastors and Teachers.

"Let another man praise thee, and not thine own mouth; a stranger, and not thine own lips." (Proverbs 27:2)

There are more self-appointed Apostles and Prophets in particular today, than there have ever been before. Men and women who, at their own discretion, have proclaimed that God has placed an Apostolic or a Prophetical call upon their lives. And they set themselves as icons within a 21st-century evangelical Body of Christ. And where is there a protest or a challenge to this self-exaltation? The very Scripture verse quoted above refutes their self-proclamation because the endorsement that is being called for does not come from within their own personal reservoir of disciples. That acknowledgement, praise, and recognition should come from those on the outside of their ministry, not the inside. And the error is not restricted to only Apostles or Prophets. The whole of the five-fold ministerial call of God is under assault.

When any church or any ministry becomes predominantly "my kingdom come" and no longer "thy kingdom come", there is cause for questioning and concern. And an ability to persuade and emotionally stir individuals to commitment is not something that is necessarily the anointing of God, as the history of David Koresh, Jim Jones, Charles Taize Russell, and Adolph Hitler reveals.

Many times with self-appointed individuals there are self-esteem and self-identification issues that are involved. The need to carry a title and be recognized becomes compulsive, and a necessity for sustaining personal value becomes a mandatory element.

Should a close examination of personal lives take place, a quagmire of disobedience, sin, and rebellion might potentially fall like skeletons from the closet onto the floor.

When you are approached by ANYONE who proclaims, "God has called me to be a prophet," or "I am an apostle of God," or "God has called me to prophetically speak to the church," or any other statement that runs along those lines, a red flag should immediately spring up from within you and the voice of the umpire should be heard as declaring, Strike One.

2. Encountering Christian 'independent agents' that do not need to belong to the local church.

Sadly, there are far too many Christians who are persuaded that they are spiritually mature. They have attended church in their early years of walking with the Lord, but now they know enough, and God has called them to be a blessing in general to the Body-of-Christ. They receive their marching orders directly from God Himself, and they feel no need to be scrutinized or held accountable to what they believe that God has directly called them to do.

They are not planted within any local church; they are not submitted unto an anointed valid minister. To them there is no such thing as NOT hearing from God. They feel that they love God, and so everything that bursts forth into their consciousness must be coming from God. They become motivated and believe that their commission is to spearhead projects and events that actually might have a valid basis within the Scriptures and are certainly good works.

Should they be challenged for their intentions or their ideas, they feel rejected. They withdraw and become very sullen. Because they are in reality, spiritually immature, they attribute the failure of what they wanted to do as being the fault and short-coming of others because they know that they heard from God.

They are not an asset to the Body of Christ, but rather a liability. And many times their behavior brings a reproach upon the name of Christ to the individuals all around them who have been led to believe that they are *godly*. And quite sadly, it is almost impossible to correct them and witness a genuine change for the better. They are locked-in to what they believe and are convinced that after all these years, and after all of the evident blessings that have come forth from God, and after all of the good that has come forth from what they have done, they could not even remotely have missed it. The problem must lie with others.

3. Encountering professed 'Bible experts' that are Biblically ignorant and spiritually void.

It is beyond count the number of times that this author has heard from various individuals, "I **know** what the Bible teaches". And without exception, the truth of the matter is that they do not **know** what the Bible teaches, on any given issue. Committing a few Scripture verses to memory or having a *common notion* of what the Bible is talking about, does not qualify anyone as **knowing** the Bible.

Most of the time these individuals are not Born-Again children of the Most High God. They are men and women of the world, who may be extremely 'nice' people, having grown up with an "I believe in God" mindset, that have been influenced along life's path with Biblical statements that have caught their attention.

"Now if any man have not the Spirit of Christ, he is none of his" (Romans 8:9b) or as Jesus said, *"Except a man be born again, he cannot see the kingdom of God." (John 3:3b)*

Within the Scriptures we find the spiritual reality of the New Birth, and the explanation that if we are not Born-Again within our spirit, then we do not have a relationship with, nor belong to, the Living God. Now that does not exempt, by any means, the Body-of-Christ from having its own fair share of Bible experts, who, in fact, are not experts at all in their knowledge of the Scriptures. Genuine Bible knowledge necessitates the ability of being able to *"rightly divide the word of truth."* (II Timothy 2:15) Sadly today, there is a tremendous amount of un-rightly divided truth running around.

The summation of the matter, for the sake of time and space, is that those who have a genuine, deep desire to learn what the word of God genuinely teaches, need to position themselves in a manner that deviates from the standard, run-of-the-mill, middle-of-the-road tradition that is out there, and away from the commandments and doctrines of men.

4. Mistaking *good intentions* with spiritual truth.

Spiritual truth does not change. The Living God that we serve does not change. The declared word of God, that we know of as the Scriptures, does not change. The power of God does not change. God's way of doing things does not change. How God thinks, does not change. What God says, does not change. How God behaves, does not change. What God has promised to do, does not change. What God says will happen in the future, does not change.

"For I am the Lord, I change not; therefore ye sons of Jacob are not consumed." (Malachi 3:6d)

Good intentions and 50 cents used to be able to buy a cup of coffee. Today, the coffee probably costs more. Good intentions will always seem to be *good*. However, if whatever intentions there may be that are put forth do not line up with the word of God, then they are of no real value no matter how well intended they are.

Flaky Christians have good intentions all the time. That is how they are able to justify, at the very least to themselves, why they do the things that they do. And they are always persuaded that what they do is "of God". Sadly, we have reached a point in Christianity where it is no longer a matter of *". . . believe on him whom he has sent,"* *(John 6:28)* but rather we feel compelled to initiate project after project after project, with the intent, one can only imagine, of pleasing God.

May the God of all grace help us to re-evaluate our own lives and the motivations behind all the things that we do 'for God'.

Spiritual warfare wise, this is a difficult place. For our own protection it would benefit us to become sensitive to, and be able to recognize, flaky Christians. We are commanded to love and remain courteous to all of the brethren, but we are not obligated to fall prey to their seductions and maneuvers.

Now . . . a flaky Christian does not have to remain a flaky Christian. Just as the Apostle Paul wrote to the believers at Rome —

"For to be carnally minded is death; but to be spiritually minded is life and peace." *(Romans 8:6)*

When an individual first receives salvation, they are carnally minded, and there is nothing that they can do about it. Spiritually speaking, a person passes from spiritual death unto spiritual life with that salvation. But at that point in time they are still worldly and carnally minded, and there is nothing that they can do about it.

At some point in time during his or her Christian walk with the Lord, an individual has an epiphany concerning their spiritual condition, and they understand and recognize that they are carnally minded. However, they do not wish to remain carnally minded because they have read within the Bible that the future of carnality is not too good. So, that person begins to read, and to meditate, and to study the word of God just like they were supposed to do right from the beginning of their walk with the Lord. That is good. They have a bright future ahead should they continue in their endeavors.

In like manner, an individual that approaches his or her Christianity frivolously can easily become flaky, and they are not even aware of the fact that they are becoming flaky. They have gone to church and read their Bible. They have even memorized some favorite verses from the Scriptures. They are able to declare Hallelujah! and are even able to 'hold their own' when a conversation arises about God. But personally, they do not like commitment. They do not like the idea of someone other than God Himself telling them what they should do. They have read in the Bible that they are at liberty now and that no man can teach them anything of real value, because they have the Holy Spirit of God as their personal teacher and mentor. They begin to become a liability to the whole of the Body of Christ instead of an asset.

However, similar to the carnally minded individual, at some point in time during their walk with the Lord they experience an epiphany concerning their spiritual condition, and they come to understand and recognize that they are flaky. They do not wish to remain flaky because they have read the back of the Book, and the end of the program does not fare well for flaky persons. So they begin to read, and to meditate, and to study the word of God in earnest, just like they should have done from the beginning. They commit themselves to a local church, and submit themselves for instruction, and continue to press in to the things that line up with the word of God, until the time appointed of the Father arrives. They are then able to go forth at the genuine leading of the Holy Spirit of grace, and truly prove to be an asset unto the Body of Christ, and the whole of the plan of God.

And in both the arena of carnality, and the arena of flakiness, effective fervent prayer is what is going to make the real difference and avail much.

Our prayer is that this work has provided some encouragement and some practical steps that can be taken in the very real warfare that we are involved with. Please prayerfully consider what has been presented, and purpose to move forward in victorious expectation for friends, neighbors, loved ones, and your own personal life's issues. God's blessing be upon you.

Maranantha, the Lord cometh.

About the Author

By-The-Book Ministries, Inc. began in 2001 as a teaching outreach. Rob Daley has been gifted by God to be able to explain biblical truths in an easy to understand manner. Many have been blessed by his teaching style.

Rob was saved and filled with the Holy Spirit in 1978 and has been instructed by the greatest teacher of all—the Spirit of Truth Himself. Rob is an ordained minister with the Assemblies of God International Fellowship and has pastored in various churches over the past 34 years.

It is the desire of this ministry to see the Body of Christ solidly taught, and grow up into the things of the Lord. Rob is available for seminars, retreats, conventions, etc.

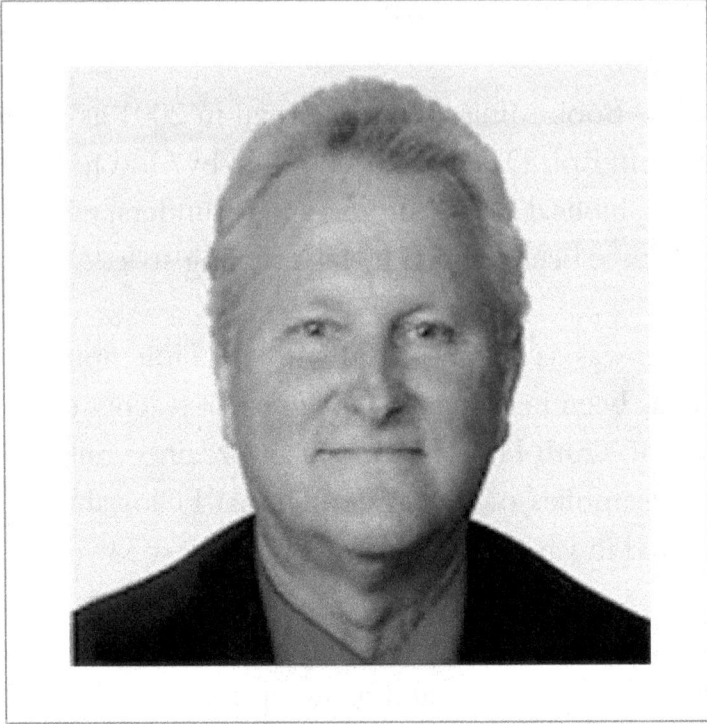

Rob can be reached at:

thedaleys@bythebookministries.org

http://robdaleyauthor.com

www.ingramcontent.com/pod-product-compliance
Lightning Source LLC
Chambersburg PA
CBHW060810050426
42449CB00008B/1613